S... McCormick

~~HHH~~ Amendli...

overactive (R) Brain - HIJ Anxiety & Depression -

(R) Big Picture - imagination Brain Depression is elevated i.e. artists "I wonder what you are thinking about me." These thoughts are elevated i.e. - mom.

Reading is a left Brain activity

To my wife Kris and my children
Daniel, Jonathan, and Kirsten
who are second only to Christ
as God's greatest gifts to me.

(L) Reality is more left Brain

Pt. w/ Anxiety & depression experience more calm w/ left Brain activated

(R) Post traumatic stress should have (R) shaded

Glasses - close (R) Brain

(L) handed people are in their (R) mind. Controls opposite side of Brain

"Gospel Therapy"

A New Vision Of Life Through Christ

An Eleven Week Study Program Addressing the Physical, Mental And Spiritual Components of Depression

Rev. Daniel Lee Krueger

Second Edition

First Printing: December 2005
Second Printing: March 2006

First Edition Published January, 2004
(Published as a three ring binder)

International Standard Book Number: 1-59872-296-4

Printed in U.S.A. by
Instantpublisher.com
PO Box 985 ~ Collierville TN 38027

To order materials or contact the author go to
http://gospeltherapy.com

Preface

The Beginning of My Passion

I am not a licensed therapist, nor do I have a Ph. D. in psychology or theology. I am a concerned Christian Pastor of the Lutheran Church Missouri Synod variety. I graduated from Concordia Seminary, St. Louis, Missouri in 1981 with a Master of Divinity and stayed for an extra year of study in Old Testament Theology. In the fall of 2002, while serving in my fourth parish, I helped bring together several groups for a conference on "Christian Care at Life's End." Along with a physician in my congregation I volunteered to lead a topic on depression at life's end.

Throughout my ministry I have counseled with individuals suffering from depression. I have seen what depression does to people, and have always known that the gospel of Jesus Christ could help in ministering to individuals who are chronically depressed or anxious.

When counseling with individuals suffering from chronic depression or anxiety, our sessions together would usually end very positively. The gospel appeared to have made a difference. However, within a few weeks, and sometimes days, the positive input that had been received would dissipate, like a drug wearing off.

Sometimes, after having sessions that ended with grateful expressions, I would later hear through the grapevine that the grateful member was now angry or upset with me. It was not until I began to study for my half hour topic that I understood why my counseling efforts were so short lived, or twisted into a negative encounter.

I became acquainted with the principles of a particular form of therapy called "Cognitive Behavioral Therapy." The essence of this therapy revolves around how you are thinking, rather than why you think in a particular way. Risking an oversimplification, the cognitive therapist doesn't care if you were abused as a child, or suffered from some tragic life experience. In battling depression or anxiety, dealing with these past experiences is not the critical issue. What matters most, is how you interpret what is happening right now.

Cognitive therapy helps people to identify thinking styles that drive us to depression and anxiety, and then teaches alternate methods for interpreting life. With modern advancements in medical imaging technology, researchers have demonstrated that simply changing a thinking pattern through therapy produces physical changes in the brain similar to changes seen in people taking medication.

Medical imaging technology has proven that depression and anxiety are not merely medical conditions that can be treated only by drug intervention. We are not simply byproducts of the brain we are born with. We can change how we think, and in so doing change the physical structure of the brain itself.

I became intrigued by the inner workings of the brain and began to research the physical processes involved in human thought. I also began a more detailed investigation of cognitive therapy. Everything I learned about the brain and cognitive therapy, and every new piece of research, was confirming that drugs combined with therapy was the most effective, longest lasting, approach to treating these human conditions.

As these ideas were transformed into certainties based on available medical research, my interest in this subject began to turn into a compulsion driven by two factors. The first factor was recognizing that many of my own members were trapped in the belief that depression and anxiety were purely medical conditions. I didn't have to take a poll to discover this.

Even before this period of intense interest I would occasionally suggest in a sermon or Bible study that the gospel of Jesus Christ might help people battle depression. Once in a while I would suggest that declining church attendance in our nation might have something to do with increasing rates of depression.

After expressing these random thoughts I would receive an angry phone call or visit from various members who were taking depression medication. They would tell me that I knew nothing about depression. Depression, they explained, was a medical condition, based on a chemical imbalance. How dare I suggest that their problem had anything to do with faith?

The second factor driving my interest was the lack of any spiritual dimension in the secular cognitive therapy books I had read. In fact, many times I would read statements from secular literature on cognitive therapy that specifically contradicted biblical ways of understanding the world.

The more I studied the more I felt compelled to do something. I felt it was intolerable to allow people to continue to suffer from depression or anxiety because they were trapped in a belief that their condition was purely medical. I became convinced that the principles of cognitive therapy, when combined with God's grace, could become a powerful tool for changing lives. What began as a half hour discussion evolved into a Bible study, a workbook, and now this book.

Reverend Daniel Lee Krueger

Table of Contents

APPENDIX

Table of Abbreviations

Genesis	Gn
Exodus	Ex
Leviticus	Lv
Numbers	Nu
Deuteronomy	Dt
Joshua	Jos
Judges	Jdg
Ruth	Ru
1 Samuel	1Sa
2 Samuel	2Sa
1 Kings	1Ki
2 Kings	2Ki
1 Chronicles	1Ch
2 Chronicles	2Ch
Ezra	Ezr
Nehemiah	Ne
Esther	Es
Job	Job
Psalms	Ps
Proverbs	Pr
Ecclesiastes	Ec
Song of Solomon	SS
Isaiah	Isa
Jeremiah	Je
Lamentations	La
Ezekiel	Eze
Daniel	Da
Hosea	Ho
Joel	Joe
Amos	Am
Obadiah	Ob
Jonah	Jon
Micah	Mi
Nahum	Na
Habakkuk	Hab
Zephaniah	Zep
Haggai	Hag
Zechariah	Zec
Malachi	Mal
Matthew	Mt
Mark	Mk
Luke	Lk
John	Jn
Acts	Ac
Romans	Rm
1 Corinthians	1Co
2 Corinthians	2Co
Galatians	Ga
Ephesians	Ep
Philippians	Php
Colossians	Col
1 Thessalonians	1Th
2 Thessalonians	2Th
1 Timothy	1 Ti
2 Timothy	2 Ti
Titus	Tit
Philemon	Phm
Hebrews	Heb
James	Ja
1 Peter	1Pe
2 Peter	2Pe
1 John	1Jn
2 John	2Jn
3 John	3Jn
Jude	Ju
Revelation	Re

Introduction

Starting Down a New Road

People often talk about turning their lives around. However, if you have been walking down the wrong road in your life, merely turning yourself around doesn't change where you are. While the Bible gives us accounts of dramatic conversions, the fact that someone started walking down a new road of life doesn't mean that all the baggage from their former life suddenly disappeared.

One of the more interesting aspects of Scripture, as an ancient document, is that there are no heroes with the exception of God. All the principal figures in Scripture make huge blunders even in the midst of their service to God. Moses never enters the promised land because of his arrogance at the waters of Meribah (Nu 20:11-12). King David commits the sins of murder and adultery with Bathsheba (2Sa 11 & 12). The same Peter who confesses that Jesus is the Christ, later denies him (Mt 26:75). No matter how hard we try to live the Christian life, sin always clings to us. The only way we can completely rid ourselves of sin is to put off our sinful nature in death.

Several times in this study we will reference one particular passage from the apostle Paul. This passage highlights the difficult struggle all Christians experience.

> (Rm 7:15-24) *"I do not understand what I do. For what I want to do I do not do, but what I hate I do. And if I do what I do not want to do, I agree that the law is good. As it is, it is no longer I myself who do it, but it is sin living in me. I know that nothing good lives in me, that is, in my sinful nature. For I have the desire to do what is good, but I cannot carry it out. For what I do is not the good I want to do; no, the evil I do not want to do--this I keep on doing. Now if I do what I do not want to do, it is no longer I who do it, but it is sin living in me that does it. So I find this law at work: When I want to do good, evil is right there with me. For in my inner being I delight in God's law; but I see another law at work in the members of my body, waging war against the law of my mind and making me a prisoner of the law of sin at work within my members. What a wretched man I am! Who will rescue me from this body of death?"*

While this book may give you new insights into the grace of God, and how you employ that grace in your life, the brain you have after reading this book will be little altered from the brain you had prior to reading it. The converted Christian always carries within his or her self the brain of a sinner. However, alongside of that old brain is a new brain, a new heart, which calls us to a new life.

Living the life of grace begins where we are at, but facing a new direction. Instead of being driven in the direction of what we must do, we are drawn by the knowledge of what God has done and will do for us in Christ. As we walk with Christ in the way he leads us, we will experience, in increasing measure, the blessings he offers of forgiveness, hope, joy, peace, and love. However, our walk on the narrow path that leads to salvation is never perfect.

One day our walk with Christ may be two steps forward and one step back. At some moments we will be intensely tuned in to the voice of Jesus calling us. The path we need to follow will seem perfectly clear. At other moments, we will be distracted by our old sinful self who never leaves us, and is constantly trying to steer us off the course of life and peace that Jesus has paved for us.

In these moments of despair we need to recall that in Jesus' death and resurrection our eternal salvation is always secure. There is no place in this life where God can not find us. There is nothing we can do from which he can not deliver us. Our salvation does not depend upon what we do, or how we feel, but upon the objective work that Jesus accomplished for us on the cross. His work, not ours, is our only hope! However, experiencing the earthly fruits of the promises Jesus makes to us is a blessing we can grow in.

Growing in God's grace involves gaining mastery over our old sinful self. Many Christians, however, feel they are losing this battle. The problem is not that God's word has failed, but that many Christians are failing to use God's word correctly. All too frequently Christians seek the power to defeat sin in the words of Scripture where God tells us what we should do.

Mastery over our sinful self is not gained through a greater understanding of the law and commands of God. Knowing what we should do does not grant us the power to do it. Our sinful nature can only be overcome by God. We can only gain the power to subdue our sinful nature by growing in our knowledge of what God has done, and learning how to apply that knowledge to more of our daily life. It is the knowledge of what God has promised to do for us in specific ways, that gives us the ability to do what God has asked.

To give a brief example, imagine yourself on your death bed, filled with fear, because you know nothing about Jesus and his free gift of forgiveness and eternal life. In that state of fear, now picture a Christian friend standing near your death bed saying, "The Bible tells us we shouldn't be afraid to die!" While this statement correctly describes how a Christian should face death, the mere knowledge of what you should do will never calm your fears.

Rather than calming a troubled heart, the idea that "we shouldn't be afraid to die" can actually increase fear. The statement suggests to the already fearful person that they don't have what it takes to be saved. Certainly the Bible tells us to "fear not," but the ability to obey the command is not found in the command itself, but the knowledge of what God has done to conquer that which we fear.

Gaining mastery over our sinful self is not accomplished by learning more about what we should do, but through a deepening understanding of what God has done and will do for us in every aspect of our life. Scripture teaches, and all the prophets and apostles demonstrated, that this process is never completed until death when we put off our old sinful nature. Nonetheless, we will experience the fruits of the Spirit in an increasing measure as we grow in our understanding of what God has done for us and how his gracious gifts are applied to our daily life.

This being the case, I doubt that the simple first reading of this book will dramatically change your life. Hopefully, however, this book will begin a process. God willing, this book will help you identify some destructive ways of thinking and set you on the path to replacing those destructive thoughts with constructive thoughts rooted in God's grace.

Changing how we think is not a one time event, but a life long and daily struggle between our sinful nature and the Holy Spirit who works in our hearts through word and sacrament. The recovery of stroke victims provides a useful point of comparison for this process.

When a person suffers a stroke, a portion of the brain literally dies. When those brain cells die, an individual loses the memories, the motor abilities, or the thinking skills that were stored or accessed through that part of the brain. The ability to walk, talk, and even to recall past experiences, can be restored. However, accomplishing this requires retraining of the brain so that it can think in a new way.

Retraining the brain to think in new ways is not accomplished through a single event. You can't restore, for instance, the use of the right hand by simply telling a person how to use it or by having that person read a book on hand movement.

Even a once per week therapy session is typically not enough to regain the loss of function that stroke victims experience. To regain the use of a limb, or to learn how to talk again, a stroke victim must go home and do daily exercise, repeating certain movements over and over again. Even into old age most people can regain at least partial function of skills that were completely gone, but it takes hard and repeated work on a daily basis.

The process of retraining can be made even more difficult if the patient can accomplish certain tasks without using the skills or abilities that were lost. Fairly recently physical therapists have discovered that stroke victims who have not regained function in an arm or leg for years can sometimes be restored to near normal function by totally immobilizing their good limb.[1]

Researches have found that functional limbs actually interfere with the therapy being applied to a paralyzed limb. The results of this immobilization of a good limb are often dramatic. What couldn't be accomplished in years of continued therapy is overcome in one or two weeks of immobilization.

Unfortunately, as we try to retrain how we think about life, we can't immobilize our sinful nature. While the voice of Jesus tenderly calls us to think in a new way, our old sinful nature is shouting at us, telling us not to listen. Our sinful nature is constantly devising all kinds of reasons and excuses, real and imagined, to keep us thinking in our old and destructive ways. While the objective word of God may tell us to go one way, the world, the devil, and our own sinful self utilize our feelings and emotions to drive us in a self destructive direction.

---

[1]Restak, Richard M.D., "The Secret Life Of The Brain" (David Grubin Production, Inc., The Dana Press and the Joseph Henry Press, 2001 p. 181-183)

Changing our thinking is a life long process, not a single event. While you may read through this book in a few settings, I believe this book is best used by those who read through it in a slow, step by step approach. For that reason I employ lesson numbers, rather than chapter headings. Each lesson should be followed by at least a week of focus where the insights gained in that lesson are incorporated into daily life.

I would also recommend that you find someone to read through this book with you. When God created Adam he said, (Gn 2:18) *"It is not good for the man to be alone. I will make a helper suitable for him."* God designed us from the very beginning to need support and encouragement from others. Frequently the way we perceive ourselves is different from the way we are perceived by others. The need for input and encouragement is not a sign of our own weakness, but a testimony to the way God designed us. God designed us to need each other!

To bring others into the process you might contact a friend who is struggling with depression or anxiety and set up weekly meetings to compare notes as you go through the book together. If you are married, have your spouse read the book also. If you belong to a church, you might consider using the lessons in this book as a group discussion outline. You could set up sessions with a pastor or counselor. However you accomplish it, connect with someone to encourage you and help you to envision a different way of thinking about your life.

Finally, I commend to you the importance of remembering the Sabbath day, as God tells us in the third commandment (or fourth depending on how your church numbers them). One of the primary reasons for attending church is to give and receive encouragement. The Bible tells us: (Heb 10:25) *"Let us not give up meeting together, as some are in the habit of doing, but let us encourage one another"*

In this regard I will share with you my own biased opinion at the risk of you closing the book and asking for a refund. I firmly believe that hope and peace cannot be built on an uncertain foundation. Jesus says,

> (Mt 7:24-27) *"Therefore everyone who hears these words of mine and puts them into practice is like a wise man who built his house on the rock. The rain came down, the streams rose, and the winds blew and beat against that house; yet it did not fall, because it had its foundation on the rock. But everyone who hears these words of mine and does not put them into practice is like a foolish man who*

built his house on sand. The rain came down, the streams rose, and the winds blew and beat against that house, and it fell with a great crash."

In much of the Christian world today the Bible is regarded as an uncertain document. In 1985 a group called the "Jesus Seminar" was organized. Consisting of biblical scholars and professors, representing numerous Christian backgrounds, this organization gathers together and votes on which words of Jesus are really the words of Jesus.

While most church bodies would label the Bible as an inspired document, there are very few that would label the Bible an "inerrant" document, specifically stating that every word in Scripture is God's word. Because of this frivolous attitude toward Scripture debates rage in the modern church over questions of human sexuality, right to life, the historical character of biblical events, and even the words of Christ.

In his earthly ministry Jesus said, (Mt 5:18) *"I tell you the truth, until heaven and earth disappear, not the smallest letter, not the least stroke of a pen, will by any means disappear from the Law until everything is accomplished."* The apostle Peter writes, (2Pe 1:21) *"For prophecy never had its origin in the will of man, but men spoke from God as they were carried along by the Holy Spirit."*

I firmly believe that God, seeing our frail human condition, would lovingly give us a clear and certain guide to the truth. Why else would he have written with his own hand on tablets of stone the ten commandments? Why else would he send his own Son into the world? In Jesus Christ (Jn 1:14) *"The Word became flesh and made his dwelling among us. We have seen his glory, the glory of the One and Only, who came from the Father, full of grace and truth."*

I feel blessed to have grown up in a denomination that treats the Bible as certain truth, rather than a document where only scholars can figure out what God's word actually means, and which words are really his words. I also believe that my church is particularly careful to make sure that the grace of God is reflected in every aspect of our teaching.

In this respect I share the observation made by one individual I have confirmed. This particular individual had studied philosophy in college, and had made the rounds through numerous denominations. Toward the end of our adult instruction classes she remarked, "You Lutherans don't leave man anything!"

The root of the Lutheran reformation may be summarized by the words from Ephesians 2:8-9 *"For it is by grace you have been saved, through faith--and this not from yourselves, it is the gift of God-- not by works, so that no one can boast."* If you consider the perspective on God's grace that I offer in this work as something unique and different from what you are accustomed to hearing, it may have something to do with the church you attend. While the applications of God's grace to the insights of cognitive therapy might be something new, the perspective on God's grace that I offer in this book is something I have been taught since childhood.

From Adam and Eve onward our sinful world has always tried to make salvation more complicated than simply depending on the gracious character of God. We're always looking for something we can do to make life better. We're always trying to make life and salvation dependent in some way on our own efforts. From what I've studied of other faith systems, I happen to believe that my church body does the best job at keeping grace as pure and simple as God intended it to be.

Too often people join churches based on relationships rather than what a church actually teaches. While Christian relationships are important, they are not what saves us. Ultimately we are saved through faith in God's word. The apostle Paul writes: (Rm 10:17) *"Consequently, faith comes from hearing the message, and the message is heard through the word of Christ."* We need regular refreshment in our faith from God's word, because our sinful nature is constantly trying to distract us and diminish our faith in the pure and amazing grace of God.

If you aren't regularly going to church for this refreshment, you should start. I don't subscribe to the prevailing attitude, "It makes no difference where you go to church, so long as you go somewhere." Different churches hold to different teachings and beliefs about God and his grace. Certain faith systems proclaim the grace of God more clearly, and with greater certainty, than others.

While I'm certain that not everyone who reads this book will share my particular bias, I hope that everyone who reads this book will start asking questions about what their church believes, teaches, and confesses. I firmly believe that hope, joy and peace in life can only be built on a foundation of certainties.

These certainties will never be found in anything we do. Our human nature is too frail and sinful to accomplish anything perfectly or with absolute dependability. Thus, our hope must always be grounded solely in the grace of God revealed in Holy Scripture. If you find yourself in a church that is reluctant to speak with certainty about this grace, or even opposes the idea of such certainty, I encourage you to find one that does.

Lesson 1

Understanding How the Brain Works

What's the Point? *This lesson is a general overview of the brain and how physical, mental, and spiritual factors influence its structures and functions. By understanding these basics of the brain and how it is influenced, we gain hope that no matter how deep our depression, our mental outlook can be changed.*

Some of you will find the first four lessons of this study program boring, and some of you will find them fascinating. Some people want to know how engines work and become auto mechanics, and other people just want the car to go when they turn on the ignition. I happen to fall into the first category.

I believe that the more you understand the biological functioning of the brain, the more importance you will attach to the principles shared in this study. The more we understand the mechanics of depression and anxiety, the better we are enabled to avoid those things that drive us to despair, and cling to those things which lift us up. We begin our journey by asking the question:

IS DEPRESSION A PHYSICAL, MENTAL, OR SPIRITUAL PROBLEM?

We all get depressed at times. Certain life events cause great sadness. Jesus himself wept at the grave of Lazarus (Jn 11:35). The hardness of the hearts of men causes Jesus grief (Mk 3:5). However, while Jesus experienced these feelings, he also could experience joy and gladness. His reaction was to a situation, and not a general characteristic of his mood. Clinical depression is different. Clinical depression alters one's ability to do work or to function socially or personally.

The standard medical definition of clinical depression requires that at least five of the following symptoms are present in the same two weeks, nearly every day, as noted by the patient or by others, and are a definite change from usual functioning. Depressed mood or decreased interest or pleasure must be one of the five.

Clinical Characteristics of Depression

1) *Depressed mood (or irritable mood if a child or adolescent).*
2) *Decreased interest or pleasure.*
3) *Significant weight loss or weight gain when not dieting or significant increase or decrease in appetite.*
4) *Insomnia or hypersomnia (excessive sleep).*
5) *Psychomotor agitation or retardation.*
6) *Fatigue or loss of energy.*
7) *Feelings of worthlessness or excessive or inappropriate guilt. This "negative thinking" usually causes a marked lowering of self-esteem and self-confidence with increased thoughts of pessimism, hopelessness, and helplessness.*
8) *Diminished ability to think or concentrate. Marked forgetfulness often accompanies this disorder.*
9) *Recurrent thoughts about death, recurrent thoughts of suicide (with or without a plan) or has made a suicide attempt.*

In addition to meeting these criteria, a major depressive disorder cannot be due to a general medical condition, substance-induced mood changes (alcohol, medication, or other drugs), bereavement, bipolar disorder, or other mood altering psychosis such as Schizophrenia or Delusional Disorder.

Depression is not just a reaction to a specific event, but a filter through which all life events pass. Clinical depression is a persistent style of thinking, a filter which alters our perception of reality in a profoundly negative way.

As we deal with this type of depression, it is important for us to answer the question, "Is depression a disease or a spiritual condition?" Do we treat it as a medical condition with pills, should we seek counseling from a therapist, or is the best prescription found in seeking spiritual renewal? Biblically, and according to modern medical research, the answer is "Yes!"

Study and Discuss

Read Mark 12:30

With what four things are we to love our Lord?

Read Psalm 31:9-10 and Proverbs 14:30

How do sorrow, grief, or envy affect our bodies?

Dealing with depression isn't a choice between physical, mental, or spiritual treatments, but includes all of these dimensions. We are not three distinct entities of body, mind, and spirit, but an integrated whole. Extreme mental and spiritual conditions impact the body, including the development and functioning of the brain. Conversely, problems with our body impact our mental and spiritual state.

The ultimate testimony to the interplay of body and spirit is the history of our relationship with God. When sin entered the world, it not only broke down a spiritual relationship with God, but it brought about our own physical death. Our redemption through Christ's suffering on our behalf is a by-product of both a spiritual and physical struggle. Jesus experiences abandonment by God (Mt 27:46) *"My God, My God, why have you forsaken me"* as well as physical death, in order to accomplish our salvation.

Unfortunately, our modern culture has attempted to divorce our bodies from the mind and spirit. Roughly 90% of those who seek help for depression or anxiety are under treated. A very typical treatment will be a single visit and prescription from a primary care physician.[2] This results in a society surviving on medications while rates of depression, anxiety, and other mood disorders are steadily increasing.

According to IMS Health, a pharmaceutical information and consulting firm, sales of antidepressants increased 73 percent to more than $12 billion from 1998 to 2002. Sales of analeptics (stimulants such as Ritalin and Adderall) increased 167 percent. This startling rise in the

[2]Howard, Pierce J. "The Owner's Manual for the Brain" (Bard Press, Atlanta & Austin, 1994,99: p. 333)

use of medications comes at a time when clinical research is demonstrating that drugs alone are not the best treatment depression.

New studies have found that combined drug therapy and psychotherapy dramatically improved the lives of patients suffering from clinical depression.[3] Separately, drug therapy and psychotherapy had very similar rates of response (55% versus 52%). However, when combined, these different approaches to the treatment of depression produced results that neither therapy could achieve on its own.

The leading researcher of the study, Dr. Martin B. Keller, noted that, *"Adding structured psychotherapy to the usual antidepressant regimen increased our response rates by 30%. Not one of us had a clue at the outset that psychotherapy would add that much . . ."* Keller found that some patients who underwent combination therapy were able to sustain pleasure and function fully at work, with families and friends for the first time in more than 20 years.

Depression is more than a chemical imbalance. The surprise of leading researchers at the success of combined therapy illustrates how deeply ingrained is the belief that depression is only a medical issue. Because of this mistaken belief, most people do not even seek spiritual counsel as a component of treating depression, and church professionals treat clinical depression as a matter for the medical community.

Combined therapy not only produces better immediate results, but also more lasting results. Several studies have shown that the relapse rate of combined therapy is substantially less than the relapse rate for people who use only drug therapy. One study found the difference in relapse rates for patients receiving combined therapy was 25% versus 80% for patients receiving drug therapy alone.[4]

---

[3]Keller, M. B., et. al, (2000). "A comparison of nefazodone, the cognitive behavioral-analysis system of psychotherapy, and their combination for the treatment of chronic depression." (New England Journal of Medicine, 342 (20), 1462-1470, 1518-1520)

[4]Fava GA, Rafanelli C, Grandi S, Conti S, & Belluardo P. "Prevention of recurrent depression with cognitive behavioral therapy: Preliminary findings." (Archives of General Psychiatry, 55:816-820, 1998)

Can the Way We Think Physically Change Our Brain?

How we think affects the physical and chemical makeup of our brains. A reporter from CNN/Time writes:

> *"the brain of a depressed person is organically different from the brain of a non-depressed person. The brain actually changes in depression. And new studies indicate there may be actual brain damage - something like scar tissue - in untreated cases of long-term depression."* [5]

Our thought patterns change the physical structure of our brains. Long term depression can do permanent physical damage. How we think is not predestined by the physical nature and brain we are given at birth. Just as muscles are shaped by the way they are used, so also our brains are shaped by how we use them. Our thoughts, behaviors, and environment all influence the physical structure of the brain.

The ways in which we change the physical structure of our brains are particularly evident in growing infants. In a May 29, 1997 interview on the PBS News Hour with Jim Lehrer, the Psychologist Geraldine Dawson from the University of Washington shared the following:

> *"Scientists have found that a baby's experiences--whether he's happy, whether he hears lots of music or speech, gets hugs and eye contact--actually change the physiological development of his brain--the quality and quantity of the electrical wiring between cells . . . What we're learning is that very early in life there are these periods when certain parts of the brain are being wired and that later in life these patterns will be very difficult to change."* [6]

More significantly for our study on depression, Dawson later commented:

---

[5]CNN.COM, "Research on depression shows genetic and chemical link", (http://www.cnn.com/ SPECIALS/1999/cnntime/sories/depression/)

[6]PBS, "Child's Play", http://www.pbs.org/newshour/bb/youth/ jan-june97/ brain_5-29.html

"What we believe is that by experiencing different emotions that you're stimulating different parts of the brain and that this then leads to connections between the synapses."

Dawson studied the difference between the brains of infants who had happy mothers and the brains of babies whose mothers were depressed. The region of the brain specialized for joy, generally the left side of the brain, showed considerable neural activity in the babies of happy mothers. The brains of children with depressed mothers looked different. Dawson continued:

"What we found was that the area of the brain that was specialized for positive emotion showed less activity and the area of the brain that specialized for negative emotion showed more brain activity. In later life an individual like this will be more apt to respond negatively when they're stressed or they experience a negative event."

Infancy may be the time of greatest change in our brain, but the brain has the capacity to change how it works throughout our entire life. As mentioned earlier, a very common demonstration of this is the recovery of stroke victims.

Stroke causes paralysis, memory loss, and makes people unable to speak, because it damages those parts of the brain responsible for those functions. In order to gain back movement or speaking skills, the brain must literally rewire itself, or change the way it thinks.

In a normal person the left side of the brain controls speech. If this area of the brain is damaged by stroke, MRI imaging techniques demonstrate that the right side of the brain takes over this function, although it must relearn the skills.[7] An interesting experiment also seems to show that the right side of the brain has the capacity to learn new language skills at roughly the same rate of a similarly aged healthy person.

The fact that stroke victims who are well advanced in years can, through intensive therapy, recover some lost skills, proves that at any age we can change or rewire the way our brain works. Age and other factors may make this process more difficult for some people, but it can

---

[7]Blasi V, and others, "Word retrieval learning modulates right frontal cortex in patients with left frontal damage." (Neuron 2002;36:159-170)

be done. An even more appropriate demonstration of this principle is a study of nuns living in Minnesota.

Since 1986, the "School Sisters of Notre Dame" in Mankato, Minnesota, have allowed themselves to be used by researchers looking for clues about Alzheimer's disease and aging. Their common life environment (they don't smoke, they are celibate, and have a similar diet) allows the researchers to rule out many variables that affect studies done on the general population.[8]

After autopsy many of the nuns exhibited all the classic physical brain damage associated with Alzheimer's. However, during their life, many of the nuns showed few, if any, changes in cognitive function. Researchers have found both physical and lifestyle reasons for this.

A low level of the B vitamin "Folic Acid" found in some nuns seemed to influence the development of the disease.[9] Folic Acid is important to brain development. A shortage of this vitamin in pregnant women causes neurological problems in babies.

This research is also showing that what we do with our mind plays an important role in how the brain responds to physical damage. A report in the June 24th, 2003 issue of *"Neurology"* shows that the more education and brain stimulating activity a person has, the less likely they are to show signs of Alzheimer's, even though autopsies revealed that their brains were physically well advanced with the disease.

David A. Bennett, MD, a neurologist with Rush Alzheimer's Disease Center in Chicago and the lead researcher of the study says that education *"may make the brain more adaptable and flexible."* The bottom line is that who we are and how we think are not mere functions of what is physically going on with our brain. Our brains are dramatically affected by our behaviors and what we choose to fill our minds with. This principle is not new, but firmly rooted in the teachings of Scripture.

---

[8]Garloch, Karen "A fascinating Study of Nuns, Alzheimers", (The Charlotte Observer, March 17, 2003)

[9]McKeown, L.A. "Low Levels of B Vitamin Linked to Alzheimer's Lesions", (WebMD Medical News Archive, New York: April 4, 2000)

Study and Discuss

Read Philippians 4:4-9

How does focusing on the good things in life affect our state of mind?

Scripture teaches that the direction and focus of our minds has a profound affect on our mood. Our mood can also be affected by our physical state. Physical pain, for instance, can put us in a negative mood and may therefore influence our mental focus. Our physical, mental, and spiritual states are constantly acting upon and influencing each other.

Stress, anxiety, and other negative thoughts trigger your brain and body to secrete certain chemicals. These chemicals, when secreted over sustained periods, have a restraining effect on the chemicals your brain uses in the positive thought process. In other words, if you don't break the cycle of negative thoughts, your mood will descend in a downward spiral, a bottomless pit from which it is difficult to emerge without help.

Someone once said, *"If you keep on doing the same things you'll get the same results."* Our life can easily slip into patterns that are destructive to our emotional well being. Without examining those patterns, and making a conscious effort to change what we are doing, it is difficult to change our overall mood.

Using the outline on the next page, briefly examine your activities in life. When you determine whether or not an activity is positive or negative, make that evaluation based on how you feel after the activity, rather than before it. For instance, I hate doing taxes, but I love the feeling I have when my taxes are done and dropped off in the mail. You may hate exercising, but always feel great after work out.

Discuss

List personal techniques or activities in each area below that may impact your mood positively or negatively.

PHYSICAL: (Work out, clean, yard work, nap, etc.)

A) activities that positively affect my mood are . . .

B) activities that negatively affect my mood are . . .

ENVIRONMENTAL: (Music, books, t.v., driving, etc.)

A) places or activities that positively affect my mood are . . .

B) places or activities that negatively affect my mood are . . .

SOCIAL: (Friends, family, co-workers, etc.)

A) people or situations that positively affect my mood are . . .

B) people or situations that negatively affect my mood are . . .

Your mood is not simply a byproduct of the chemical makeup of your brain. The choices you make in physical activities, environment, social settings, and how you interpret all these events, combine together to alter your mood. These choices actually change the chemical and physical structure of your brain.

From a biblical viewpoint, our eternal salvation hinges on God's ability, through the message and work of Christ, to change how we think. The familiar biblical word "repent" literally means "change your mind" (from the Greek words "meta" *change* and "noieo" *consider, perceive, or think*). While the Christian faith results in a changed lifestyle for the believer, this new life is ultimately rooted in a new way of thinking rooted in God's grace to us through Jesus Christ.

Study and Discuss

Read Jeremiah 31:31-34

Why did the old covenant God made with Israel fail?

How will God change Israel so that the new covenant will not fail?

Read Romans 12:2

What change must take place in order for us to be able to understand God's will?

Read Mark 1:14-15

What kind of news does Jesus bring to us?

What change occurs with those who repent?

Repentance is not simply being sorry for something you have done wrong. Repentance is a new way of thinking focused on the "good news" we have in Jesus Christ. Lessons 4-11 of this study will focus on specific ways that we can more effectively incorporate this good news into our daily living. The next two lessons, however, will focus primarily on the physical and life style changes we can make as components in the battle against depression and anxiety.

Lesson 1 ~ Weekly Activities

If you are stressed as to whether or not you have answered the questions properly in this lesson, I do give some suggested answers to all the lesson study questions in the Appendix. For the supplemental readings in the "Weekly Activities" there are no suggested answers except the ones you suggest while doing your personal devotions.

You may want to read on, but I think you are better off stopping at the end of this section. Let a week pass before you move on to the second lesson. Talk about what you have learned with friends. Take time to absorb and reflect upon what you have read. Overcoming depression and anxiety involves permanent changes in the way we live and think about our lives. These changes take time and effort.

CARING FOR THE BODY AND SPIRIT GOD GAVE ME

To help you stay focused throughout the week every lesson includes some review material, some devotional reading, and other activities. Each week the amount of work will intensify until lesson 5.

In the **Appendix** (pages A3 - A8) you will find a guide for tracking such things as sleep, diet, exercise and devotional time. While we will explain and focus more on these factors in future lessons, it is important to begin paying attention to these aspects of your life now by completing this form each day.

SCRIPTURE READING

The major emphasis in the weekly activities for this first lesson is to begin cultivating your devotional life. We will start out with some devotional reading and questions. Each evening read a part, perhaps a chapter, of Paul's letter to the Philippians. While you are reading Paul's letter, answer the following questions.

According to chapter 1:7, and 1:13-17, what is Paul's earthly situation?

What seems to be Paul's mood as you read through this letter (see verses 1:3-4, 1:18)?

What potentially negative situations does Paul describe in the following verses?

a) 1:13

b) 1:15, 17

c) 1:20-22

How does Paul put a “positive” spin on the negative situations listed above?

a) 1:14

b) 1:18

c) 1:23-25

While negative events abound in life, where does Paul want us to focus our thoughts according to Philippians 4:8?

What is the result of a life focused on God’s blessings according to Philippians 4:9?

What is the secret to Paul’s contentment in life according to Philippians 4:11-13?

Having read through Paul’s letter, would you say that Paul could find plenty of reasons to be depressed about life?

What is different about Paul that allows him to be so joyful about his present life circumstances?

- NOTES -

- NOTES -

Lesson 2
Brain Chemistry and the Effects of Drugs, Diet, and Exercise

What's the Point? *By understanding the chemical makeup of the brain and how these chemicals function, we realize the important role that drugs, diet, and exercise play in how we think and respond to the world. Caring for the body God gave us is very important in battling depression.*

When teaching this material, many people find this lesson to be the most complex and difficult to grasp. While you may struggle with this material, it is important to understand the effects of what we do with our bodies and what we put into our bodies. With that understanding comes a greater appreciation for how drugs can help us, but also a greater appreciation for what drugs can't do, and the side effects they can cause.

As you read through this material please understand my own limitations. My expertise is not chemistry, nutrition, or physical therapy. In addition to these limitations the advancements in brain research are happening so fast that long held beliefs are frequently tossed out and new theories of brain function take their place. What I've written here may be outdated by the time you read it. With these basic qualifications here goes my best attempt to help you understand some brain basics.

How Do Chemicals Influence the Brain?

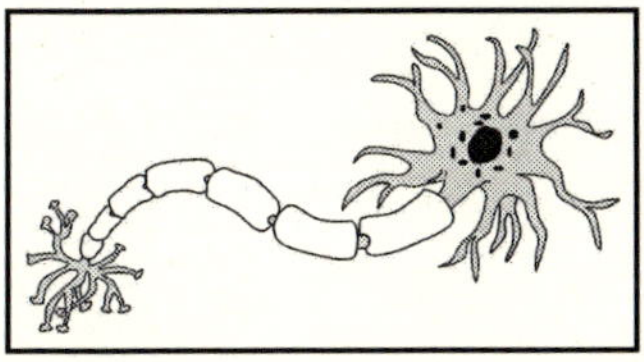

Meet the **neuron**, the type of cell that makes up your nerve fibers and your brain. At birth you possess roughly 100 billion brain cells. The number of cells is not as significant as the number of connections that they make to other cells, and the strength of those connections.[10]

The impulses inside of a neuron travel electrically from the cell body (large part called the "soma") to the cell end (small part called the "axon

[10]Pierce, p. 44

terminal"). The "myelin sheath" is a coating of fat that encircles the axon (long part). This sheath insulates the electrical signal within the neuron and helps the signal travel faster and farther.

With a healthy myelin sheath the electrical signal inside of a neuron can travel up to 100 meters per second. Without myelin, the signal slows to about 1 meter per second. In the absence of this sheath the neurons are essentially short circuited and incapable of transmitting messages.

When we are born, the spinal cord and the areas of the brain responsible for instinctive behaviors have an intact myeline sheath. At birth an infant's brain weighs about 300-350 grams (⅔ to ¾ lb.). The adult brain weighs about 1200-1500 grams (2 ⅔ to 3 ⅓ lbs.). Virtually all of this weight and size increase is due to the process of myelinating the rest of the brain cells. I presume that God designed things to work this way so that babies wouldn't go stir crazy being cooped up in a mother's womb for nine months, and to ease the process on mom when delivering a newborn.

Shortly after birth the visual and auditory centers of the brain are myelinated, followed by the motor areas of the brain. Myelination of the brain continues into the early twenties. The last parts of the brain to be fully myelinated are the frontal lobes (logic centers), which is why mature logical judgment only develops with age. Thus, our cognitive development roughly parallels the myelination of our brain neurons.

Neurons range in size from less than a millimeter to more than one meter in length. The healthy composition of the fatty myelin sheath is essential to the proper function of the brain and nervous system. The break down of this sheath is what occurs in the disease "Multiple Sclerosis." As this disease progresses, the insulating character of this sheath is changed. The electrical impulses traveling from one end of the neuron to the other either don't arrive, or arrive too late, to properly coordinate with other cells. Later in this lesson we will discuss how diet can profoundly affect the health of this myelin sheath.

The little fingers surrounding the large part ("soma") of the neuron are called "dendrites". One neuron can have thousands of these dendrites with their tiny branches. It is through these dendrites that a neuron receives information from another neuron. While the neuron talks from one end to the other electrically, the conversation between

99% of all neurons is initiated by chemicals received by the dendrites called "neurotransmitters."

Until recently most researchers believed that we had all the brain cells we could ever have on the day we were born. Modern research has shown that we have a limited capacity to grow new brain neurons even into old age.[11] Neural growth and shrinkage is particularly evident in the in the hippocampus (a critical area for understanding depression), the olfactory (smell) bulb, and possibly in areas of the cortex.

Not only can we grow new neurons, but individual neurons are constantly growing and pruning the dendrites and axon terminals that are used as neurons talk to each other. Simply by reading this book, you are changing the physical structure of your brain.

The capacity of the brain to change itself physically has introduced a new caution into medical research of the brain, especially when trying to determine cause and effect relationships between brain structure and human thought. In other words, it is an increasingly open question if a particular physical characteristic of the brain causes someone to think or act in a particular way, or if the way in which a person thinks or acts changes the physical characteristics of their brain.

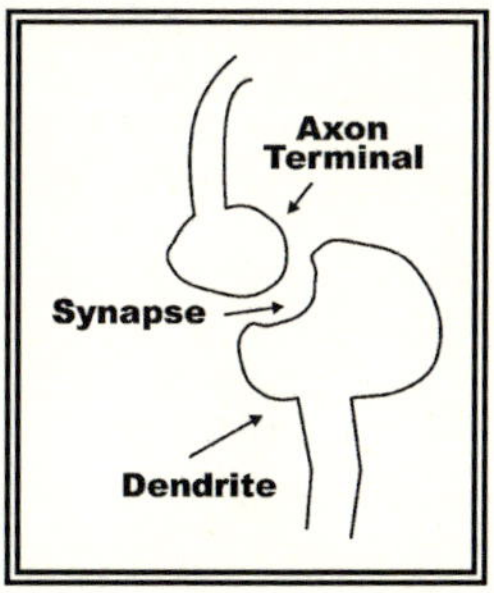

When a neuron talks, it doesn't fire all of its axon terminals at once. One or more of the axon terminals will release a specific chemical or neurotransmitter into a tiny gap between itself and the dendrite of a neighboring neuron. This gap is called a "synapse." When the amount of neurotransmitter in the synapse reaches a certain threshold, the neighboring neuron will pick up the message and process it in an appropriate way. If the signaling axon terminal doesn't put enough neurotransmitter into the synapse, the message will be lost.

For many years it was thought that each neuron released only one type of neurotransmitter, but modern research has shown that individual neurons can release several types of neurotransmitters. Together with

[11]Dayer, A.G.; Cleaver, K.M.; Abouantoun, T.; Cameron, H.A., "New GABAergic interneurons in the adult neocortex and striatum are generated from different precursors" (Journal of Cell Biology, 2005 168: 415-427. Published Jan 31 2005)

other aspects of neuron function, one single neuron can transmit literally thousands of distinct messages.

In some ways the learning process is not so much the ability to accumulate information, but the ability to ignore certain information. At any given moment your brain is receiving input from all of its senses. Without the ability to turn the volume down on some of the those messages, and turn up the volume on others, concentration would be impossible.

As we learn, we teach our neurons when to speak with a loud voice, softly, or not at all. Thus, as neurons signal other neurons, there is a certain threshold of chemical signaling that must be met before the other neuron responds. Diet, sleep, drugs, mental and physical stress levels, gender hormones, and countless other factors influence this chemical signaling process.

The chemical signaling process between neurons gives rise to the common description of depression or anxiety as the result of a chemical imbalance. This description, while accurately describing the disruption of proper brain function that is characteristic of these mood disorders, unfortunately communicates nothing with regard to how the process becomes disrupted.

If an obituary notice for a 30 year old person who smoked 10 packs of cigarettes a day, lived off beer and french fries, slept 4 hours every night, worked in a high stress job, never exercised, and used cocaine stated, "died of a heart attack," it would accurately reflect the immediate cause of death, but wouldn't even begin to reflect the real causes of this individual's untimely demise. In the same way, while the chemical signaling process of the brain does not function properly in depression, anxiety, and other mental disorders, describing them as the result of a chemical imbalance says nothing about how this imbalance is created.

As the neuron communicates, it doesn't waste the chemicals it uses. Some of the chemicals used in brain messages are reabsorbed by the neuron after a message is sent. The neuron's ability to reabsorb brain chemicals it has already used is very important in understanding how most antidepressant drugs work.

By slowing down the process of reabsorption with antidepressants, leaving more residual neurotransmitters in the synapse, the neuron doesn't need to release as much new neurotransmitters in order to get a message through to the neighboring neuron. The effect of antidepressants is similar to adding an amplifier to the voice of someone who speaks very softly.

Eventually, neurotransmitters that are not reabsorbed have to be removed. There are specific brain chemicals that are responsible for cleaning up these leftovers. The break down of this process plays a role in the development of Alzheimer's. A few older antidepressant drugs work by slowing down this process.

While there are more than 60 identified neurotransmitters that the brain uses, there are several that are extremely significant in the study of the brain and are the primary targets of modern drug therapies. These chemicals play a dominant role in the regulation of the other brain chemicals.

Endorphins

The word "endorphin" literally means "morphine produced within" and is one of several opiate type chemicals produced in the brain. The opioids and their receptors are closely associated with pathways in the brain that are activated by painful or tissue-damaging stimuli. These chemicals are released in the presence of pain, exercise (producing the runner's high), or eating hot chili peppers. Relaxation exercises can also trigger the release of these chemicals.

When flooded with opiate drugs such as heroin and morphine the brain may stop producing its own natural opiates.[12] Over time more drugs are required to achieve the same effect. Severe withdrawal symptoms persist until the body recovers its ability to produce its own opioids. Alcohol and nicotine also suppress the body's natural production of these chemicals. As a result, people who stop drinking or smoking suffer withdrawal symptoms.

Dopamine

The neurotransmitter "Dopamine" plays a significant role in muscle movement. The brains of people with Parkinson's disease have virtually

---

[12]Meyers, David G., "Exploring Psychology" (Worth Publishers, NY:NY, Fifth Edition, 2002, p. 37)

no dopamine. Their muscles tense up and their movements become jerky and uncertain.

Increased levels of dopamine have a stimulative affect. They increase heart rate, circulation, metabolism, and our ability to do concentrated mental work. The presence of dopamine also encourages the release of endorphins (see above) which produce euphoria. Until recently excessive dopamine had been implicated in Schizophrenia, but recent research has suggested that the role of dopamine and other neurotransmitters in this disease is much more complex than indicated by earlier research. Children with ADD were formally thought to have insufficient dopamine in a certain brain area, but the latest research actually indicates that the real culprit is insufficient serotonin in their systems. Low serotonin levels are also the main chemical deficiency linked to depression.

Dopamine's release is stimulated by cocaine and amphetamines (speed). These drugs can also stimulate the production of serotonin. Thus, the attention levels of ADD, ADHD children are increased by the use of amphetamine drugs like Ritalin or Adderall which stimulate both dopamine and serotonin. These drugs also inhibit the ability of the body to "clean up" excess dopamine. Repeated use of these drugs or alcohol diminishes the body's own ability to produce these chemicals. Thus, over time there is a need to increase the use of drugs and alcohol to achieve the same effect.

Acetylcholine

"Acetylcholine" was the first neurotransmitter ever identified. It is used in muscle fibers to stimulate contraction. One of its functions is to stimulate glands. Normally, acetylcholine is quickly removed after having performed its action. Nerve agents block the removal of this transmitter resulting in continuous stimulation of the muscles, glands and the central nervous system. Certain insecticides prevent the production or use of acetylcholine producing paralysis and death.

Acetylcholine helps maintain the health of the cell membranes of neurons. It is manufactured from dietary fat. In Alzheimer's patients there is a shortage of acetylcholine in the brain.

Norepinephrine (or noradrenaline)

"Norepinephrine" is released in the brain during emotional or exciting situations. It plays a significant role in fixing memories by creating strong and lasting connections between neurons (synapses). Rats who are deprived of this chemical can learn new information but cannot retain information for any significant period. This chemical also plays a role in regulating heart rate and blood pressure.

GABA (gamma aminobutyric acid)

"GABA" functions as a dampening system for unwanted brain input. It allows you to tune in the ball game and tune out the people talking around you; that is, until you hear your wife ask, "Did you take the garbage out?" Without GABA, concentration would be nearly impossible.

GABA levels decrease with age, making it more difficult to focus intently. Certain tranquilizers such as Valium, Xanax and Librium work by boosting levels of GABA in the brain. GABA can be purchased as an over-the-counter dietary supplement.

Serotonin

In our understanding of depression and anxiety "Serotonin" is one of the most significant brain chemicals. Serotonin and its derivatives are used by the portions of the brain that regulate hunger, thirst, mood, breathing, sleep, confidence, perspective, self esteem, empathy, attitude and many other things. Low serotonin levels are present in people with depression and ADHD, many sleep disorders, FMS (Fibromyalgia) and obesity. Elevated serotonin levels have been associated with Chronic Fatigue Syndrome and Autism. Because of this brain chemical's strong link to depression, we will spend more time understanding how it works.

How Do Drugs Affect Serotonin Levels?

There are at least 14 different neuron receptor types for serotonin. In other words, what serotonin accomplishes depends upon what part of the brain, what neuron, and what synapse you are talking about. This is why drugs that raise serotonin levels often have negative side effects, such as producing abnormal blood pressure.

You can't raise serotonin levels in your brain through a serotonin injection or by taking a pill with serotonin. The brain has a barrier between itself and the blood which carries nutrients. The "blood-brain barrier" prevents toxins or excessive levels of nutrients from disrupting normal brain function.

There are three basic ways to raise serotonin levels. One way of increasing serotonin levels is to stimulate your brain and increase the speed with which it creates neurotransmitters. Another method of controlling serotonin levels is to slow down the reabsorption of serotonin by the neurons. Finally, you can slow down the process of breaking down unabsorbed serotonin. There are numerous mechanisms behind these processes, but our first focus will be on drug therapies.

Current drug therapies for depression and anxiety all raise serotonin levels by preventing either the destruction or the reabsorption of serotonin your brain has already made. Currently there are no pharmaceutical drugs that help the brain selectively manufacture more serotonin without also speeding up the manufacturing of other brain chemicals.

The initial connection between drugs and depression was found by accident in the 1950s. During that time period two groups of drugs were discovered that had the side effect of combating depression. One class of drugs was used to treat tuberculosis. These drugs are referred to as **Monoamine Oxidase Inhibitors (MAOIs)**. Another class of drugs came from the quest to treat allergies and produce tranquilizers. They are referred to as **Tricyclic Antidepressants (TCAs)**.[13]

Monoamine oxidase is an enzyme in your body that breaks down two neurotransmitters: serotonin and noradrenaline. It is one of the ways that your brain cleans up left over serotonin that was not reabsorbed by the neurons. The **MAOIs** prevent this enzyme from doing its work. Phenelzine (Nardil) and sertraline (Serlin) are examples of this type of drug.

---

[13]Lader, Malcomb OBE, "The Biology and Treatment of Clinical Depression" (April, 2002 http://www.channel4.com/science/microsites/S/science/body/depression.html)

Female sex hormones also influence MAO activity. Progesterone tends to increase MAO activity (reducing serotonin levels) and estrogen tends to decrease MAO activity (raising serotonin levels). This why women often have monthly mood cycles, and why hysterectomies, pregnancy, birth, or menopause can produce profound changes in mood.

When monoamine oxidase is suppressed, numerous side effects can occur. This same enzyme breaks down amines from foods like cheese and yeast in the stomach. MAOIs allow amines in those foods to enter the blood circulation system, causing a potentially dangerous rise in blood pressure. Consuming a large amount of caffeine can also produce this extreme effect, along with some medicines used in cough and cold remedies. Because of these side effects, MAOIs are now usually reserved for severely ill patients who have failed to respond to other antidepressants.

TCAs work by preventing the reabsorption or re-uptake of serotonin and noradrenaline. Until fairly recently these antidepressants, known as imipramine (Tofranil), amitriptyline (Elavil), prothiaden (Dothiepi), and nortriptyline (Pamelor), were the main form of drug therapy for depression. These drugs also block the re-uptake of acetylcholine, causing side effects such as dry mouth, constipation and blurred vision. They also have an antihistamine effect and can create a feeling of sedation and "spaceyness." Thinking, attention, concentration and memory may be poor. Hunger for sweet foods is also increased. Since these drugs block the re-uptake of noradrenaline they may cause low blood pressure. Sitting patients can faint if they stand up quickly.

The newer antidepressants are called **SSRI**s, short for **selective serotonin re-uptake inhibitors**. These drugs are fluoxetine (Prozac), paroxetine (Paxil), citalopram (Celexa) and sertraline (Zoloft). Though not yet perfect, these drugs are more selective, as the name implies, in blocking the re-uptake of serotonin and therefore cause fewer side effects than earlier drugs. Still, these drugs are not selective in terms of the region of the brain they affect.

While modern antidepressants may improve mood, they can also negatively impact other areas of your brain influenced by serotonin levels. This will depend not only upon the drug being used, but the patient's own neuro-chemistry. Such symptoms may be nausea or loss of appetite, loss of sexual desire, tremors and a rise in anxiety levels.

There are also some withdrawal symptoms associated with SSRIs. These might include poor coordination, fatigue and dizziness.

As you can see, using drugs to alter serotonin levels is not a great solution to depression. Additionally, all the current drugs do nothing to help your brain produce serotonin. The positive effect of drugs is achieved by preventing existing serotonin from being destroyed or reabsorbed. The real question we need to answer is how does the body normally maintain proper serotonin levels?

How Do Gender Hormones Influence the Brain?

For a long time researchers have known that women are twice as likely to suffer from depression as men. However, until recently, there has been relatively little research studying depression in relationship to gender specific biology. Recent studies have shown that the brain is profoundly influenced by gender hormones.

Estrogen increases the ability of the brain to both retain and to utilize serotonin. As mentioned earlier, one of the effects of estrogen is that it blocks the work of monoamine oxidase (MAO) which cleans up excess serotonin and noradrenaline. Thus, estrogen not only increases serotonin levels, but also increases norepinephrine activity in the brain.

Estrogen also increases the number of the receptors that make use of serotonin in the brain, particularly in the right prefrontal cortex and hippocampus. In other words, certain neurons grow when estrogen is present in the body, and shrink when it is not present.

A 2003 study on the effects of estrogen showed that women receiving HRT (estrogen/progestin) therapy had a greater ability to sustain directed attention, to inhibit inappropriate responses, and to switch cognitive functions.[14] Verbal fluency, as an example, increased in women taking HRT and remained the same in those not receiving HRT.

Studies which have examined the effectiveness of treating depression with an estrogen supplement have yielded positive results for

---

[14]Kugaya A, Epperson CN and others, "Increase in prefrontal cortex serotonin 2A receptors following estrogen treatment in postmenopausal women" (American Journal of Psychiatry 2003, 160: 1522-4)

women entering or having gone through menopause, women having severe mood swings associated with their menstrual cycles and women following childbirth. Women who have normal estrogen levels do not benefit from estrogen supplements as a treatment for depression.[15]

Progesterone, as mentioned earlier, seems to accelerate the work of MAO in your brain. Women who use a progesterone only type of birth control pill are at a greater risk for depression. The natural alteration of estrogen and progesterone in a woman is an underlying cause for the familiar monthly mood swings.

Because these hormones so profoundly change both serotonin levels, and the size/number of neurons that use serotonin, women who suddenly stop ERT (estrogen only) or HRT therapy, or women who have had a recent hysterectomy, will often experience significant changes in mood tending toward severe anxiety or depression. While the brain can, in time, adjust to these changes in hormone levels, the sudden loss of these hormones in women can be compared to a drug addict going through withdrawal.

This kind of sudden change in hormone levels also occurs following pregnancy. During pregnancy the placenta itself produces additional estrogen and progesterone. The levels of these hormones can increase 50 to 100 times during the nine months of pregnancy. However, when the placenta is ejected, the hormone levels in a woman's body immediately begin to fall back to their original levels. While this sudden change does not affect all women in the same way, it does serve as the trigger in some women for the condition known as "postpartum depression." Diet during and after pregnancy may play a significant role in why some women develop this condition and some do not.

There are concerns with the long term side effects of ERT or HRT which make them unsuitable as a permanent treatment for depression or anxiety.[16] Estrogen replacement therapy (ERT), or unopposed estrogen, greatly increases the risk of endometrial (uterine) cancer and is not recommended for women who still have a uterus. ERT also appears to

---

[15]Muriel Darniche, BSc Pharm, and others, "Estrogen and Depression" (NS Atlantic Psychopharmacology Quarterly, Spring 1999)

[16]Victoria Hendrick, M.D, "Hormones for Perimenopausal and Postmenopausal Depression" (Psychiatric Times January 2004 Vol. XXI Issue 1)

increase problems with the gall bladder. HRT, which includes both estrogen and progestin, has been linked to an increased risk of heart disease and breast cancer.

Since these are long term side effects there is no reason, in normal circumstances, to suddenly halt these therapies. Ceasing such therapies should normally be a gradual process over several months or even a few years. This gives the brain time to adjust to the diminished hormone levels and naturally increase its serotonin production.

Testosterone, which is present in small amounts in women and larger amounts in men, breaks down in the body to estradiol, a form of estrogen. Ultimately, testosterone will have some of the same positive effects on serotonin levels as does estrogen.

In addition to stabilizing mood, hormone therapies have other positive side effects. Estrogen helps bones absorb calcium and therefore has a positive effect on bone loss in older women. Estrogen also raises HDL (good) cholesterol and lowers LDL (bad) cholesterol thus lowering the risk of heart disease.

How Does Diet Affect Serotonin Levels?

The body manufactures serotonin from tryptophan. Tryptophan is an amino acid or protein. Your body can manufacture many different amino acids but tryptophan is not one of them. Thus, tryptophan is referred to as an **"Essential Amino Acid."** If your diet doesn't include foods that have this protein, you will eventually die for lack of it. If your diet is low in this protein, or your diet makes it difficult for your body to use this protein properly, you will have lower serotonin levels.

Tryptophan is particularly found in milk, yogurt, eggs, meat, nuts (peanut butter), sunflower seeds, beans, fish, and cheese. Among the cheeses cheddar, gruyere, and Swiss cheese are particularly rich in tryptophan. Spinach and raw mushrooms are also very high in tryptophan and make a great salad. Among the meats, turkey has one of the highest tryptophan levels. Though tryptophan can be obtained from many common foods, simply eating a meal containing these foods will not automatically raise your serotonin levels.

Tryptophan can't get into the brain all by itself. Tryptophan needs another molecule to help it get from the blood stream into the parts of the brain where it is manufactured into serotonin. The problem is, when you are eating foods containing tryptophan you are also consuming many other amino acids. There are five other amino acids (leucine, isoleucine, valine, tyrosine and phenylalanine) that all compete for the use of these "transporter" molecules that are used by tryptophan to cross the blood-brain barrier so that it can be manufactured into serotonin.

Picture the other amino acids as a crowd of people trying to catch a taxi after some major event in New York. Tryptophan is just one face in the crowd. The larger the crowd the harder it is for tryptophan to catch a ride. During a normal meal with a variety of foods it will be very difficult for tryptophan to obtain the necessary transporter molecules to get to its destination in the brain. The other amino acids preoccupy all the transporter molecules.

Richard and Judith Wurtman, researchers from the Massachusetts Institute of Technology, have shown that meals high in carbohydrates can actually help tryptophan enter your brain. When you eat a food high in carbohydrates, your body releases insulin. Insulin helps clear the competing amino acids from your blood. However, insulin has no effect on tryptophan. Consequently, once insulin has cleared the competing amino acids from your blood, tryptophan is free to enter your brain.[17]

This mechanism for creating serotonin may explain a number of diet-depression connections. For instance, diabetics have a higher incidence of depression. Part of this increased risk for depression may be due to the fact that insulin in their bodies is absent or at reduced levels. Sustained higher blood sugar levels would mean, using the earlier analogy, that tryptophan faces more competition for transportation to the serotonin production plant.

You feel tired after eating a high carbohydrate meal because your serotonin levels are boosted. Dr. Albert Stunkard, a professor of psychiatry at the University of Pennsylvania, thinks that people with an almost uncontrollable urge to raid the fridge late at night are helping

[17]Wurtman, R.J & J.J., (1995) "Brain serotonin, carbohydrate-craving, obesity and depression" (Advances in Experimental. Medicine and Biology 1996; 398:35-41)

themselves to sleep by boosting serotonin levels through the consumption of food.[18]

Excessive consumption of carbohydrates found among the obese may be an attempt to self-regulate serotonin production and improve mood. The diet drug "Fen-Phen" was extremely effective in helping people lose weight. One of its primary effects on the body was to boost serotonin levels. Unfortunately, it also produced severe side effects which led to it being pulled from the marketplace.

People who quit smoking frequently gain weight. Since nicotine is a stimulant, it causes the brain to increase production of serotonin and other neurotransmitters. When nicotine is removed from our system, the brain encourages us to find another method to boost our serotonin production. Eating, particularly eating carbohydrates, satisfies the brain, but punishes the body with extra weight.

Dieting can also lower our brain's ability to manufacture serotonin. For instance, a high protein and low carbohydrate diet increases the competition for transporter molecules. Proteins are very high in the other amino acids that compete with tryptophan for transportation. Since insulin is only produced in response to sugars and starches, the body doesn't clear the competition for transportation. Studies show that after several weeks of these types of diets serotonin levels typically fall.

Tryptophan is also used by your body to construct other useful substances such as Niacin (Vitamin B3). The body manufactures Niacin in the liver and requires 60 mg of tryptophan to make 1 mg of Niacin. If you are deficient in this essential B vitamin, your body may use up the available tryptophan in manufacturing this vitamin and not leave enough available for serotonin production. Poor diet or poor liver function in the elderly, drug addicts, alcoholics, and people with liver disease, are risk factors for deficiency in this vitamin.

Deficiencies in several other B complex vitamins, such as B1 (thiamine), B6 (pyridoxine), B12, and Folic Acid have also been associated with depression. Vitamin B6 and vitamin C (ascorbic acid) are critical components in the process of manufacturing serotonin and

---

[18]Stunkard, AJ; Grace, WJ; Wolff, HG; "The night-eating syndrome: a pattern of food intake among certain obese patients" (American Journal of Medicine 19:78-86; 1955)

other neurotransmitters. Deficiencies in any of these vitamins can contribute to lower serotonin levels and the accompanying depression.

Even if you are taking a multivitamin or eating a balanced diet, it is possible you are not receiving a sufficient amount of vitamins. To begin with, most of the government's recommended daily allowances (RDA) of these vitamins are established by the amount of these vitamins necessary to prevent diseases. For example, the disease of scurvy is caused by insufficient vitamin C in the diet. While the government's RDA may reliably prevent disease, it does not necessarily represent the body's optimum requirement of these vitamins. Even if you are exceeding the RDA through diet or supplements, other factors may prevent you from making full use of your vitamin intake.

In general, caffeine, nicotine, and alcohol tend to diminish the body's resources of these vitamins. Caffeine in particular prevents your body from absorbing vitamins from food. An unbalanced diet, alcohol abuse, or the use of oral contraceptives tends to deplete vitamin B6. The ability to absorb vitamin B12 diminishes with age and the elderly are prone to this type of deficiency. If you are suffering from depression, particularly if you have any of the risk factors just mentioned, you may want to consult a physician and consider having some blood work to check for these deficiencies, correcting them with the appropriate vitamin supplement.

Certain mineral deficiencies have also been linked with depression. Manganese is very critical in the body's ability to make use of B complex and C vitamins to construct amino acids such as serotonin. Manganese is often labeled the "brain mineral." Even when taking vitamin supplements, a deficiency in manganese would prevent the body from making adequate use of its vitamins.

One of the most significant recent discoveries regarding diet and depression concerns the level of Omega 3 fatty acids. Because fats play such a significant role in the discussion of diet, particularly in the American culture, we will spend more time discussing the link between fat and depression.

What Is the Relationship of Fats to Brain Health?

Most people know that there are different types of fat, but don't understand the difference between a saturated fat, unsaturated fat or a trans-fat. Fats are carbon-based acids compounded with glycerine. Fatty acids can have chains of carbon atoms that are short (less than 8), medium (8-12) or long (13 +). The first short-chain fatty acid is none other than vinegar (acetic acid).

The molecules of all fatty acids are made up of two parts. At one end of the fat molecule is an acid group of atoms which is water soluble. At the other end of the molecule are carbon and hydrogen atom groups that are oil soluble. Most of us are familiar with three basic types of fats: Saturated, Mono-unsaturated, and Poly-unsaturated. The following diagrams show how atoms are arranged in these different types of fats.

0=Oxygen H=Hydrogen and C=Carbon

Figure 1

```
        0     H H H H H H H H H H H H H H H
        ||    | | | | | | | | | | | | | | |
HO  -   C  -  C-C-C-C-C-C-C-C-C-C-C-C-C-C-C-H
              | | | | | | | | | | | | | | |
              H H H H H H H H H H H H H H H
```

The fat molecule in **Figure 1** is called a **Saturated fat**. Specifically it is Palmitic Acid (16:0). The name "Saturated" refers to the fact that all of the carbon atoms in this fat chain have matching hydrogen atoms. Thus, these molecules are very stable and rigid. These fats are less likely to break down (go rancid) and are usually solid at room temperature.

Figure 2

```
        0     H H H H H H H     H H H H H H H H
        ||    | | | | | | |     | | | | | | | |
HO  -   C  -  C-C-C-C-C-C-C-C=C-C-C-C-C-C-C-C-C-H
              | | | | | | | | | | | | | | | | |
              H H H H H H H H H H H H H H H H H
```

The diagram in **Figure 2** is that of a **Mono-unsaturated fat (MUFA)**. The carbon atoms of this fat molecule are not completely saturated with hydrogen atoms. Since only one hydrogen atom is missing, this is identified as a mono (one) unsaturated fat.

The particular mono-unsaturated molecule shown above is "Oleic" (18:1 n9) acid. Because of the missing hydrogen atom, these molecules are not as stiff as the saturated fats. Typically they are fluid at room temperature. However, at refrigerated temperatures, they will become semi-rigid. This fat molecule is prevalent in many oils such as olive oil, canola oil, sesame oil, and high-oleic safflower oil. They are generally healthier for you because they do not stiffen or harden in your blood stream.

A third fat receiving a great deal of attention lately is **"Trans-fat."** While small amounts of these fats occur in nature, the vast majority are artificially produced.

Figure 3

```
     O   H H H H H H H H   H H H H H H H H
     ||  | | | | | | | |   | | | | | | | |
HO - C - C-C-C-C-C-C-C-C=C-C-C-C-C-C-C-C-C-H
         | | | | | | |   | | | | | | | | |
         H H H H H H H   H H H H H H H H H
```

Trans-fats are produced by pumping hydrogen into unsaturated vegetable fats. This process destroys some of the healthy fats (like Omega 3 fats) and stiffens the fat molecule by altering the position of the hydrogen atoms. The same fat shown in **Figure 2** (Oleic acid) is altered by this process to become the fat shown in **Figure 3**.

These trans-fats are common in processed foods and stick margarine (sometimes referred to as "Oleo"). They have a longer shelf life than their natural counterparts and are semisolid at room temperature. This makes "trans-fat" ideal for baking.

Since the molecular structure of trans-fat is so similar to natural unsaturated fats, everyone presumed these fats were healthier than eating saturated animal fats. These fats are now known to be the worst possible fats for you and are rapidly being removed from the western food chain. Apparently, it's not nice to fool mother nature.

The molecule in **Figure 4** is a **Poly-unsaturated fat (PUFA)**. These fats have more than one section of carbon atoms linked to only one hydrogen atom. In other words, there are multiple (poly) places that are not saturated with hydrogen. This makes these molecules very flexible even at cold temperatures.

Figure 4

```
     O   H H H H H H H     H     H H H H H
     ||  | | | | | | |     |     | | | | |
HO - C - C-C-C-C-C-C-C-C=C-C-C=C-C-C-C-C-C-H
         | | | | | | | | | | | | | | | | |
         H H H H H H H H H H H H H H H H H
```

The molecule in **Figure 4** is "Linoleic acid" or LA (18:2 n6). It is referred to as an Omega 6 polyunsaturated fat because the first gap in hydrogen occurs at the sixth carbon atom from the right. It has 18 total carbon atoms with 2 unsaturated links. It is particularly prevalent in oils of cottonseed, soybean, peanut, corn, sunflower and poppy seed, safflower, black walnut, pine nut, and sesame.

Figure 5

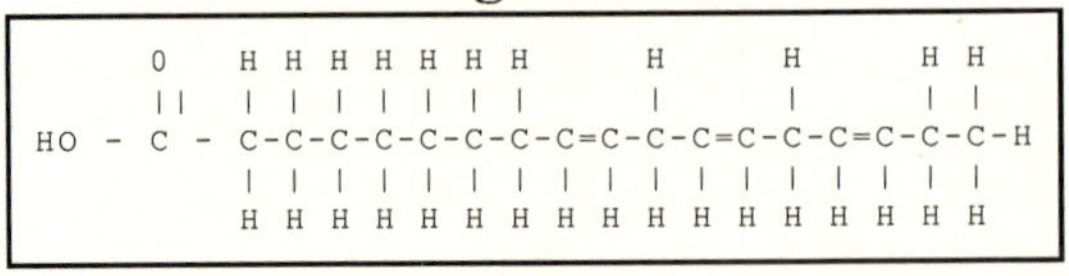

The molecule in **Figure 5** is “alpha-linolenic acid” or ALA (18:3 –3). It is referred to as a polyunsaturated Omega 3 fat because the first gap in the hydrogen atoms occurs at the third carbon atom from the right. It has 18 carbon atoms with 3 unsaturated links. Omega 3 oils are particularly important to brain health. One of the primary sources of Omega 3 oils is cold water fish (Omega 3 fats won’t get stiff in cold water).

All mammals, including humans, lack the enzyme systems to make Omega 3 or Omega 6 fatty acids. Our body can make saturated fats all by itself from sugars and starches, but these Omega 3 and Omega 6 fatty acids must be eaten in order for us to survive. Thus the Omega 3 and Omega 6 fatty acids are called **“Essential Fatty Acids**.”

If your diet doesn’t include foods that have these fats, you will eventually die from a lack of it. Linoleic acid (an omega-6) and alpha-linolenic acid (an omega-3) are the only true “essential” fatty acids because the body can build the other omega fats it needs once it has these building blocks. However, manufacturing these fats from the building blocks is both slow and inefficient.

Where are these fatty acids used? Particularly in the case of Omega 3 fatty acids, they are used to build a fatty coating and the cell membranes that surround all of the neurons that comprise your brain and nervous system. As mentioned earlier, the disease “Multiple sclerosis” is essentially a break down of this fatty coating. The portions of your brain that lack this fatty coating at birth are essentially nonfunctional.

The process of coating the brain neurons with myelin occurs rapidly from birth to six years, but is not fully completed until we are in our twenties. At maturity, 60% of your brain structure is fat. DHA, an Omega 3 fat, is the most prevalent fat in your brain.

If a diet is out of balance in its consumption of fats, the cell membranes of your neurons will become stiff and will be less able to absorb or release material, including neurotransmitter chemicals. The government recommends a diet that has a ratio of 2:1 or 3:1 of Omega 6 fatty acids to Omega 3 fatty acids. The typical American diet is 15:1 to 20:1. There is no other area of the American diet where we are more unhealthy.

Not surprisingly, rates of depression are significantly lower in populations that consume a large amount of fish.[19] A recent study published in the *"American Journal of Psychiatry"* [20] showed that people suffering from major depression often improved significantly after three weeks of receiving fish oil supplements compared to groups receiving only a placebo. Six out of ten patients improved receiving the fish oil, while only one in ten reported improvement on the placebo. Another study published in the *"Archives of General Psychiatry"* showed a roughly 3:1 improvement in the depressive symptoms of patients taking Omega 3 supplements compared to those on a placebo.[21]

Postpartum depression, more than any other form of depression, seems to be linked with deficiency in Omega 3 fatty acids. While a woman is pregnant and nursing she must not only have sufficient Omega 3 fats to maintain her own neuron health, but must supply sufficient Omega 3 fats to grow an entirely new brain and nervous system. Studies do show that women's brains actually shrink during pregnancy.[22] While not proven, some theorize that this shrinkage is to due to the loss of these essential fatty acids.

Marine fish (tuna, salmon, etc.) and leafy green vegetables are the primary sources of these fats in our diets. These fats (oils) are essential

---

[19]Hibbeln JR, "Fish consumption and major depression" (Lancet 1998; 351(9110):1213

[20]Nemets, Boris, M.D; et. al, "Addition of Omega-3 Fatty Acid to Maintenance Medication Treatment for Recurrent Unipolar Depressive Disorder" (American Journal of Psychiatry 159:477-479, March 2002)

[21]Peet, Malcolm; Horrobin; David F. "A Dose-Ranging Study of the Effects of Ethyl-Eicosapentaenoate in Patients With Ongoing Depression Despite Apparently Adequate Treatment With Standard Drugs", (Archives of General Psychiatry 2002 59: 913-919)

[22]Oatridge, A; Holdcroft, A; et. al, "Change in brain size during and after pregnancy: study in healthy women and women with preeclampsia" (American Journal of Neuroradiology; Jan 2002; 23(1):19-26)

in maintaining the flexibility of cell membranes. Dietary saturated fats which are dominant in our American diet, or are manufactured by our bodies when we over eat, pack together and become very stiff. They are dangerous to cells, especially artery walls where they will harden and plug our blood vessels. Diet can play a significant role in our overall brain health. Any plan to combat depression should include a careful evaluation of diet and the use of common substances such as alcohol, caffeine, and nicotine.

In addition to diet there is another body component to good brain health. Exercise!

How Does Exercise Affect Serotonin Levels?

In a 1999 study at Duke University 156 patients diagnosed with major depressive disorder (MDD) were assigned to three groups: exercise, medication, or a combination of medication and exercise. To the surprise of the researchers, after 16 weeks all three groups showed similar and significant improvement in measurements of depression.[23] The exercise was 30 minutes on a stationary bicycle three times a week. Follow up studies seemed to show that exercise also enhanced general cognitive ability. These results have been confirmed by separate studies.

One theory behind the benefit of exercise is that through increased blood flow the brain is stimulated and has more energy to do its work. Another boost from exercise may be the burning of competing travelers trying to catch a ride to the serotonin factory. By burning off food molecules in the blood stream the level of tryptophan entering the brain is increased thus allowing the brain to manufacture more serotonin.

Another reason for the benefit of exercise is that it actually encourages the growth of neurons particularly in the hippocampus area of the brain. This area of the brain tends to shrink in depression and tends to grow as mood improves. Still another possible reason for the beneficial effect of exercise may be that it lowers our overall stress level.

---

[23]Blumenthal, James A. PhD, “Exercise Treatment for Major Depression” (Psychosomatic Medicine 2000; 62:633-638)

At least 50% of all people clinically diagnosed with depression have an abnormal level of the stress hormone "cortisol" found in their blood.[24] Aerobic exercise (sustained lower level activity) seems to be the exercise best suited to provide these benefits.

Planning Life Style Changes

Most of you won't remember the names of the neurotransmitters or their functions as discussed in this lesson. Most of you will probably forget the precise mechanisms by which hormones, diet, and exercise affect the brain. However, by reading through this material you hopefully gained a sense of the intricate relationship between what we do with our bodies and how we think.

Our mind, body and spirit are not separate entities. God created us as one person with body, mind, and spirit intimately related and constantly affecting each other. What we do with our bodies through diet and exercise can have a profound impact upon our mind and spirit.

Before implementing any of the following suggestions you should always consult with a medical professional. You should NEVER stop or start taking a prescribed medication without consulting a physician.

Even simple vitamin supplements and certain foods can interfere with the proper functioning of medications. For example, if you are on blood thinners, a vitamin E supplement or the consumption of foods high in vitamin E can cause excessive bleeding. Omega 3 fats, while being generally healthy, have the effect of lowering your inflammation response. If you are a person with a compromised immune system, a diet high in Omega 3 fats may further dampen your immune response.

Before you consider implementing any of the following suggestions, you should consult with a physician. That point being emphasized, the following general statements may be made.

1) Numerous studies demonstrate that diet and exercise can have as significant an effect upon depression as taking prescription medications. Like drugs, diet and exercise can improve our brain chemistry. Therefore:

---

[24]UCSF News Office, "Recent Research Suggests New Strategy for Treating Depression," (Sept. 20, 1999, http://pub.ucsf.edu/newsservices/releases/2004010628/)

a. prior to starting a prescription program for depression and anxiety you should pursue diet and exercise changes in consultation with a physician.

b. If you are taking medication for depression or anxiety, diet and exercise may enhance the effects of drug therapy and ultimately eliminate the need for them. Again, talk to a physician before making any changes.

2) Hormonal imbalances can also alter brain chemistry. Younger women suffering from severe mood swings during the month, women with hysterectomies, and women entering or beyond menopause may want to further investigate hormonal therapies with a physician. Because of the serious side effects from these therapies, they should be approached with extreme caution.

3) You may want to have a physician do some blood work and check for any vitamin deficiencies. For most healthy people, taking a multivitamin per day is probably useful. This vitamin should include a healthy dose of B-Complex and some minerals such as Manganese. Elderly people in particular should be concerned about their intake of B-complex vitamins since the ability to process these vitamins decreases with age. Deficiencies of Vitamin B are more commonly associated with depression symptoms in the elderly.

4) Virtually all Americans are deficient in Omega 3 fats in ratio to the Omega 6, saturated, and trans-fats we consume. Closely evaluate what kind of fats you are eating. Eat butter instead of margarine, cut down on the consumption of fried foods, and consider taking an Omega 3 supplement (usually fish oil). One gram per day of the Omega 3 fats of EPA and DHA (usually 3 fish oil tablets), seems to have been therapeutic in the studies conducted on depression and Omega-3 supplements. This is not only good for brain health, but heart health, skin health, and possibly certain forms of diabetes. Again, if you have any health issues (including being pregnant) check with your physician first.

5) Consider mild, aerobic exercise (brisk walking, riding a stationary bike, etc.) 30 minutes a day at least three times a

week. If you have not exercised for a long time, you should work toward this as a goal over several weeks.

6) Consider having one meal a day that consists of dark green leafy vegetables (spinach), mushrooms, or other foods rich in tryptophan, combined with a light course of carbohydrates (a banana, mandarin oranges, raisins, whole wheat bread). Use an olive oil dressing or some light dressing made up primarily of carbohydrates rather than a dressing high in fats or proteins. Particularly people who are on blood thinners should be careful about diet changes and should consult a physician first in these matters.

By the way, before you do any of this it is a good idea to TALK TO A PHYSICIAN. Throughout my ministry I've heard many stories from members who had some minor health issue, changed their diet, started taking vitamins, started exercising, and ended up compromising their health, because they didn't understand the full effects of the changes they were making. Just because something is good for most people, doesn't mean that it is good for you.

Having given all the warnings I can, I still encourage you to begin planning a diet and exercise routine. Find a partner that you can work out with or do dietary planning together. Even if you can't work out with someone, find a partner to report to. Call or visit with them at least once a week to discuss your progress. Ask them to give you encouragement and a gentle nudge when you are not meeting the goals you have set for yourself.

As mentioned in Lesson 1, it is important to monitor your progress. Use the appropriate material in the appendix for this purpose.

Lesson 2 ~ Weekly Activities

Take a break from reading now. If you read this chapter in one sitting you are probably worn out, especially if you tried to understand every bit of information that was presented. Let a week pass before you continue with lesson 3, but do begin focusing on some healthy changes in your life style.

If you haven't had a good physical lately, now might be the time to schedule one with a physician. Get some blood work done and discuss any diet or exercise changes you might be planning.

After you've rested your mind a bit, come back to the lesson and review the information that has been presented particularly on diet and exercise. Based on what you learned from this lesson, make a list of three healthy menu ideas for Breakfast, Lunch, and Supper. To help you research nutritional values in food, take a look at the website "www.nutritiondata.com."

Healthy Breakfast Ideas

1)

2)

3)

Healthy Lunch Ideas

1)

2)

3)

Healthy Supper Ideas

1)

2)

3)

Now put together a shopping list. You might include on that list some vitamin/mineral supplements or Omega 3 supplements. Don't forget to find foods that are rich in Tryptophan.

Now is also a good time to begin planning an exercise schedule. Take a look ahead at the next two weeks and write down 6 time periods where you could squeeze in at least a 30 minute walk or some other appropriate exercise. Write a note with these times and put it on your refrigerator or put these times in your planning calendar.

EXERCISE PERIODS FOR THE NEXT TWO WEEKS (3 EACH WEEK)

This Week	**Next Week**
1)	4)
2)	5)
3)	6)

Think about a support partner. Identify someone you can share your diet goals with and possibly exercise with. To help you track your progress, use the pages in the **Appendix** entitled:

CARING FOR THE BODY AND SPIRIT GOD GAVE ME

Though this week's material does not have a great deal of scriptural references, you should continue with some devotional reading of Scripture. Each evening read one of the following Psalms: Psalm 144 through Psalm 150. These are Psalms of praise that will help you to remain focused on the blessings we enjoy from God.

- NOTES -

Lesson 3

The Affects of Lifestyle and Activities on Our Minds

What's the Point? *Activities and lifestyle choices profoundly influence, and are influenced by, a depressed mood. This lesson identifies activities and lifestyle choices that can either deepen or combat depression. These choices not only change our momentary mood, but in time can fundamentally change our brain structure and function.*

Read And Respond Without Discussion

You are being interviewed for a job and are asked to fill out a personality evaluation. You are told that being hired for this particular job will be greatly influenced by the personality profile provided by this evaluation.

One week later you are told that you have gotten the job. When you meet again with your new employer you are told that three people evaluated your personality and you are allowed to read their evaluations. One evaluation is very positive, one is neutral, and one is very negative. After reading all of their evaluations you are told that you can meet with one of the three evaluators.

1) **Which evaluator would you like to meet with and why?**

2) **As quickly as you can, silently write down two weather related words that begin with the letter "S".**

3) **As quickly as you can, silently write down two words associated with "Life".**

How Can Our Life Style Change the Brain?

As discussed in previous lessons we are not three separate entities of body, mind, and spirit, but one person with body, mind, and spirit constantly interacting and influencing each other. Daily routine, activities, and the relationships we share with friends and relatives, can profoundly change our biology and brain structure.

Active minds can delay the onset of Alzheimer symptoms even when the biological damage to the brain is profound. Infant minds are trained by their social interaction with family members. Depressive behavior around infants actually affects their brain development making them more prone to depression in later years.

Social dominance in rat populations changes the size of the hippocampus in rats, even when stress levels remain neutral. In other words, simply where you see yourself in a social pecking order may alter the physical structures of your brain.[25] This effect seemed to be confirmed by a recent study on social status and depression. Men who experience a downward social shift are four times more likely to experience depression than men who have improved their social status. Women in the same study seemed unaffected by changes in their social status.[26]

Our relationships and activities change the way we think and feel in amazing ways. For instance, male testosterone levels are lowered by such things as marriage and the holding of a baby. [27] One fascinating study showed that when a married man simply thinks about getting his wife pregnant, his testosterone levels change to match his wife's fertility, whereas a married man who is not thinking about getting his wife pregnant, has no discernable pattern to his testosterone levels.

---

[25]Kozorovitskiy, Yevgenia and Gould, Elizabeth Gould, "Dominance Hierarchy Influences Adult Neurogenesis in the Dentate Gyrus" (The Journal of Neuroscience, July 28, 2004, 24(30):6755-6759)

[26]Tiffin, Paul A; Pearce, Mark S; Parker, Louise Parker; "Social mobility over the lifecourse and self reported mental health at age 50" (Journal of Epidemiology and Community Health 2005; 59: 870-872)

[27]Gray PB, Kahlenberg SM, Barrett ES, Lipson SF, Ellison PT, 2002, "Marriage and fatherhood are associated with lower testosterone in human males," (Evolution and Human Behavior 23:193-201)

Women who have close contact (living together, sports activities, etc.) will have their menstrual cycles synchronize.[28] Recent studies have now found that puberty is accelerated in young girls by the presence of a non-biologically related male (as in the case of stepfathers).[29]

While all the mechanisms involved in these changes are not universally agreed upon, animal and human studies indicate that many of these effects are influenced by pheromonal (scent) cues that humans give off. The bottom line is that in extremely subtle ways our biology is impacted by the company we keep. Social associations and interactions can physically alter who we are!

Stress is also an important factor influencing depression. As mentioned earlier, at least 50% of all people clinically diagnosed with depression have an abnormal level of the stress hormone "cortisol" found in their blood.[30]

Cortisol and other stress hormones are useful to our bodies in emergency situations. They increase our body's ability to use energy, they sharpen our attention, and also dampen certain bodily functions that are not immediately useful, such as our immune system. However, when our bodies are in a prolonged state of stress, these useful effects of stress hormones begin to damage our body including the structures of the brain. Recent studies show that prolonged stress actually shrinks the hippocampus, an area of the brain involved in regulating such things as mood, learning, and memory.[31]

In the battle against depression it is important to look into our daily routines, activities, and relationships to determine if they are contributing to our depressive mood. Depression has a strong negative influence on our choice of activities which tends to deepen depression.

---

[28]Stern K., McClintock MK. "Regulation of ovulation by human pheromones." (Nature 1998 Mar; 392(6672): 177-181)

[29]Ellis, B. J., & Garber, J. (2000) "Psychosocial antecedents of variation in girls' pubertal timing . . ." (Child Development, 71, 485-50)

[30]UCSF News Office, "Recent Research Suggests New Strategy for Treating Depression" (Sept. 20, 1999, http://pub.ucsf.edu/newsservices/releases/2004010628/)

[31]Brown ES, Rush AJ, McEwen BS. "Hippocampal remodeling and damage by corticosteroids: implications for mood disorders." (Neuropsychopharmacology, 1999; 21(4): 474-84)

Making a determined choice to change our daily activities can help to improve our mental outlook. Even when our outward circumstances cannot be changed, we can make fundamental changes in how we interpret or deal with certain events and lower our stress response.

HOW DOES DEPRESSION INFLUENCE ACTIVITIES?

Earlier you were asked to read and respond to a situation regarding a job interview. You were asked which personality evaluator you would prefer meeting with: very positive, neutral, or negative? This scenario approximates an experiment where a number of college students were given what they thought was a personality profile questionnaire, but its actual function was to identify students who were suffering from mild to severe depression and students who were not depressed.[32]

Figure 5

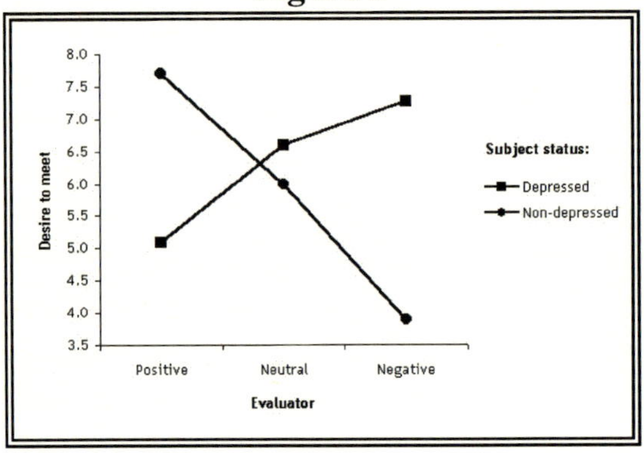

After a week the students were called in and given the results of their "personality profile." The results were actually three bogus personality evaluations: one positive, one neutral, and one negative. Everyone received the same three evaluations.

After reading each evaluation the students were told they could meet with one of the evaluators and discuss their profile.

As you can see from the graph in Figure 5, those who had been identified through the profile as depressed, were most interested in meeting with the negative evaluator. Those who had been identified through the profile as not depressed, were most interested in meeting with the positive evaluator. The experiment provides a fascinating example of what psychologists call "mood congruent behavior."

---

[32]Swann, W. B., Wenzlaff, R. M., & Tafarodi, R. W. (1992). "Depression and the search for negative evaluations: More evidence of the role of self-verification strivings" (Journal of Abnormal Psychology, 101(2), 314-317)

Logic would say that if you are in a bad mood you should choose behaviors and activities designed to improve your mood. Unfortunately, human behavior tends to run contrary to logic. Many experiments verify this effect that depression has upon our choices.

In word association experiments depressed people will more frequently give words such as "death" and "struggle" when asked about "life," whereas non-depressed people will tend to associate words such as "freedom" and "love."[33] When asked to name the first kind of weather that comes to mind beginning with the letter "S," depressed people tend toward words like "stormy" or "snowy" whereas non-depressed people typically pick "sunny" or "springtime."[34]

In an experiment where people were placed into a sad or happy mood and then shown a series of slides which could be viewed at their own pace, happy people spent more time looking at happy scenes, whereas sad people spent more time looking at sad scenes.[35] Another experiment had depressed and non-depressed students interact socially, frequently switching partners, and then rating how much they liked the other individual.[36] The old proverb "Misery loves company" turned out to be true. Depressed people preferred the company of depressed people, whereas happy people preferred the company of happy people.

In combating depression what you need to do, and what you choose to do, are often at odds with each other. This fact is reflective of our sinful condition which the Bible describes as slavery. No one wants to be depressed, but the choices we make often push us deeper into depression. The apostle Paul writes of the spiritual struggle we have against sin:

---

[33]Bower, G. H. (1981). "Mood and memory." (American Psychologist 36: 129-148)

[34]Mayer, J. D., Gaschke, Y. N., Braverman, D. L., & Evans, T. W. (1992). "Mood congruent judgment is a general effect." (Journal of Personality and Social Psychology, 63, 119-132)

[35]Kelley, C. (1982). "Some effects of mood on attention and memory." (Ph.D. Thesis, Stanford Psychology Department, Stanford University)

[36]Locke, K. D., & Horowitz, L. M. (1990). "Satisfaction in interpersonal interactions as a function of similarity in level of dysphoria." (Journal of Personality and Social Psychology, 58, 823-831)

(Rm 7:18-19) *"I know that nothing good lives in me, that is, in my sinful nature. For I have the desire to do what is good, but I cannot carry it out. For what I do is not the good I want to do; no, the evil I do not want to do--this I keep on doing."*

What kind of choices are you making in your life that contribute to depression? There are several key areas where medical research has demonstrated that specific behavioral changes can have a profound impact in the battle against depression and anxiety. In many cases the impact is as great as placing a person on medication.

How Can Lack of Sleep Affect Our Brain?

Sleep patterns and depression are closely related because the body hormone involved in regulating sleep is derived from serotonin. Melatonin is the hormone of sleep regulation and is produced by the brain's pineal gland from serotonin. This production process seems to be regulated by exposure to light.

When you are exposed to high levels of light, melatonin production decreases and you seem more awake. When you are exposed to low levels of light, melatonin production increases and you feel more tired. This biological mechanism is responsible for people feeling more depressed in winter than in summer. SAD or "Seasonal Affective Disorder" is the term given to this condition when it becomes oppressive. Treatment for this disorder is simply exposure to high intensity light.

Research has linked persistent insomnia with the onset of another major depressive episode within one year, and sleep complaints are a reliable predictor of future relapses. A 2004 study from the University of Massachusetts, Boston of 2,259 students aged 11 to 14 found that a sleep deficit was associated with lower self-esteem and higher levels of depressive symptoms.[37]

The modern American culture works against sleep. Before electric lights the average person slept about ten hours a night. Today the

---

[37]Rhodes, Jean et. al, "Sleepless in Chicago: Tracking the Effects of Adolescent Sleep Loss During the Middle School Years" (Child Development Volume 75 Issue 1:84; January 2004)

average person sleeps about seven hours per night. One third of us sleep less than six hours per night. Many factors, both social and physical, can affect our sleep patterns.

One physical cause of sleep deprivation is "Sleep Apnea." This is a condition where the airways are restricted during sleep causing oxygen deprivation and frequent waking during the night. Even though the individual may sleep several hours, they feel exhausted because they have not gotten the right kind of sleep.

Proper sleep has five phases: 1, 2, 3, 4, and REM (rapid eye movement) sleep. Half of our sleep time should be spent in stage 2 and about 20% in REM sleep. Stage 1 is light sleep where we drift in and out of sleep and can be awakened easily.

When we enter stage 2 sleep, our eye movement stops and our brain waves become slower, with occasional bursts of rapid waves called sleep spindles. In stage 3, extremely slow brain waves called delta waves begin to appear, interspersed with smaller, faster waves. By stage 4, the brain produces delta waves almost exclusively. It is very difficult to wake someone during stages 3 and 4 which are sometimes referred to as deep sleep.

During deep sleep, growth hormone is released in children and young adults. Many of the body's cells also show an increased production and reduced breakdown of proteins during deep sleep. This time period of sleep seems to be the main time period for repair in the body and the brain. Activity in the parts of the brain that control emotions, decision-making processes, and social interactions, is greatly reduced during stages 3 and 4. Without these stages of sleep it may be difficult for people to maintain balanced emotional and social functioning while they are awake.

During the last stage of sleep (called REM sleep) our breathing becomes more rapid, heart rate increases, blood pressure rises, and our eyes jerk rapidly in various directions. When people awaken during REM sleep, they remember dreams.

It takes about 70 to 90 minutes to enter REM sleep. A complete sleep cycle takes about 90 to 110 minutes. Because it normally takes a long time to enter REM sleep, brief naps do not typically allow a person to catch up on this critical sleep period.

As the night progresses REM sleep increases in length while deep sleep decreases. At the end of a good night's rest most people are spending nearly all of their sleep time in stages 1, 2, and REM. It is the lack of REM sleep that is most predictive of people slipping into depression. In animal studies, deprivation of REM sleep has the most profound negative affect on both behavior and life span.

During REM sleep a number of neurotransmitter changes take place in the brain. For instance, a chemical signal is sent to your spinal cord essentially shutting down most signals to your body. Therefore, even though your mind may be acting out many scenarios, your body remains motionless. The eyes, however, are unaffected since their nerves do not go through the spinal cord. That is why the eyes appear active during this period of sleep.

During REM sleep the neurons that contain acetylcholine, slip into high gear. Serotonin and adrenal type neurons seem to shut down. From Lesson 2 we learned that acetylcholine helps maintain the health of the cell membranes of neurons. In Alzheimer's patients there is a shortage of acetylcholine in the brain. Not surprisingly, researches have recently noticed that sleep apnea seems to be a risk factor for Alzheimer's.[38]

One of the current theories about REM sleep is that it helps us consolidate information and fix memories. Information that is acquired while we are awake is reactivated within the hippocampus during REM sleep. People taught a skill and then deprived of non-REM sleep can still recall what they learned after sleeping. However, when people are taught a skill and deprived of REM sleep, they cannot recall what they learned. The hippocampus is the same area of the brain, as noted in previous lessons, that tends to shrink during depression and grows when people are recovering from depression.

Stress, foods, medicines, and many other factors affect our sleep patterns. Caffeinated drinks (coffee, soda), diet pills and decongestants stimulate some parts of the brain and can cause insomnia. Many antidepressant drugs suppress REM sleep (which is counter productive to their intended effect on mood). Alcohol may help you fall asleep, but

[38]Conger, Krista, "Stanford researchers identify gene associated with sleep apnea" (Stanford Report, June 13, 2001)

it also reduces REM sleep time. Smoking reduces REM sleep and has the further negative effect of causing people to awaken after 3 or 4 hours of sleep due to nicotine withdrawal.

Age, gender, and individual differences make it difficult to determine the exact amount of sleep that any one person requires. Generally as we get older, we need less sleep, and when we are younger we need more. Poor sleep patterns are, however, very characteristic of depression. The following are some generally recognized ideas that promote good sleep patterns.

1) Avoid caffeine, nicotine, and alcohol for four to six hours before bedtime.
2) Don't exercise within 4 to 6 hours of bedtime. Working out earlier in the day usually improves sleep.
3) Structure your day so that in the hour before going to sleep you have some relaxation time. You might take a warm bath, listen to relaxing music, or eat a light snack.
4) The worries of the day must be set aside. Consider having some devotional or prayer time before sleep where you consciously work at laying the burdens of the day into the hands of the Lord.
5) Reserve your bed for sleeping. Don't watch television or do work in bed.
6) If you can't fall asleep within 15 to 20 minutes, rather than trying harder to fall asleep, get out of bed and read a book or do some other relaxing activity. When you are more relaxed, go back to bed.
7) Have a consistent bed time and waking time, even on the weekends. Our bodies have a natural rhythm and react negatively to shifting sleep patterns as evidenced by the phenomenon of "jet lag."
8) Avoid napping during the day since it will confuse your normal sleep pattern. Napping isn't a solution to lack of sleep, but a symptom of a chaotic and dysfunctional sleep pattern.
9) If you snore or feel exhausted even after a long night's rest you may want to consult a physician with regard to sleep apnea.

Implementing all of the suggestions above may seem like an insurmountable task in the hectic American life style. In the family situation you may need the cooperation of several people to make these changes happen. It is important to remember, however, that God designed us to sleep.

Even before sin entered the world, God used the deep sleep of Adam as the opportune time to remove a rib and make him a wife (Gn 2:21). On the seventh day of creation God rested (Gn 2:2). In the third commandment, based on this creation event, God commands us to rest on the seventh day (Ex 20:11). Scripturally speaking, proper rest is not only a gift of God, but can be a reflection of our priorities in life and our spiritual relationship to our Lord.

Study and Discuss

Read Psalm 127:1-2 and Ecclesiastes 5:10-12

What does a lack of sleep suggest about our priorities?

Read Proverbs 3:21-26 and Ecclesiastes 2:22-26

How does trust in God affect our ability to sleep?

Read Isaiah 30:15-16

Where is our salvation found?

What prevents Israel from experiencing God's salvation?

Here is the bottom line. You cannot win the battle against depression without healthy sleep. The life style, spiritual, and physical challenges that prevent you from getting a good night's rest must be changed. We are one person, body, mind and spirit. Rest for a weary spirit cannot be achieved without rest for a weary body.

How Can Talking Affect Mood?

One of the major divisions of the brain is the left hemisphere and the right hemisphere. For most people, the left side of the brain controls speech. Strokes in this area of the brain often affect the ability to talk, but these strokes also have led scientists to discover some interesting aspects of human emotion.

Damage to the left side of the brain is often associated with a negative mood, including symptoms of uncontrollable crying and other indicators frequently associated with depression. By contrast, damage to the right side of the brain is often associated with more positive mood reactions.[39] Modern medical imaging techniques have confirmed what was previously known only through observation.

The left prefrontal cortex seems to be associated with neural circuits that are more important for positive emotions. In one experiment people were shown a series of pictures that differed in their emotional content. Repeatedly showing more negative or more positive images over a period of time produced a change in mood. Using PET scans researchers have shown that positive mood changes resulted in increased blood flow to the left side of the brain, whereas negative mood changes showed greater activity in the right side of the brain.[40]

The left side of the brain is not only more active in positive emotions, but also has a dampening effect on negative emotions. Negative emotions originate deep within the brain in a region called the amygdala. People who have more activity in the left prefrontal area of the brain recover faster from negative stimulation.[41]

A recent experimental study that takes advantage of this fact consisted of placing special goggles over the eyes of people. Each eye

---

[39]Robinson, R.G.; Starr, L.B.; Price, T.R.; (1984) "A two year longitudinal study of mood disorders following stroke: revalence and duration at six month follow-up." (British Journal of Psychiatry 144: 256–262)

[40]Sutton, S.K., et al. (1997) "Asymmetry in prefrontal glucose metabolism during appetitive and aversive emotional states: an FDG-PET study." (Psychophysiology, 34: S89)

[41]Larson, C.L., S.K. Sutton & R.J. Davidson. 1998. "Affective style, frontal EEG asymmetry and the time course of the motion-modulated startle" (Psychophysiology 35: S52)

sends visual information to the right and left side of the brain. However, information from the left field of vision (for both eyes) is sent to the right side of the brain and information from the right field of vision (for both eyes) is sent to the left side of the brain.

People who have surgically severed right and left brains (a technique which treats severe epilepsy), when shown a picture to the left field of vision, cannot verbally describe what they are seeing. The image goes only to the right brain, but speech is normally located in the left brain. When the image is then shown to the right field of vision, split brain patients can easily describe what they are seeing.

Dr. Frederick Schiffer, a Harvard Medical School psychiatrist, constructed goggles that completely blocked vision to one eye and covered the inner 50% of the field of vision for the other eye. This made either the right or left hemisphere of the brain more active than the other. When his patients wore the goggles for just a few minutes, they would often exhibit profoundly different moods and even personalities depending upon which field of vision was being covered.

In one study of this effect, 71% of patients suffering from major depression reported significant (20% or more) increases in anxiety when looking through the goggles. In 73% of those patients, the increased anxiety occurred when looking through the goggles that activated only the right brain (left field of vision).

Interestingly, patients diagnosed with post-traumatic-stress disorder (rather than depression) experienced a very similar change in mood (78%) using the goggles. However, the vast majority of those whose mood became more anxious (71%) did so when the left brain (right field of vision) was more active.[42]

If you would like to try this experiment, simply purchase two sets of safety goggles from any hardware store. The goggles should cover both the front and sides of your eyes. Using duct tape or black paint, cover completely the vision to one eye, and the inner ½ to ⅔ of the other eye

---

[42]Schiffer, Fredric MD, "Can the Different Cerebral Hemispheres Have Distinct Personalities? Evidence and Its Implications for Theory and Treatment of PTSD and Other Disorders" (Journal of Trauma & Dissociation, Vol. 1(2) 2000, The Haworth Press, Inc., p. 83-104)

on one set of goggles. Repeat this procedure with the second set of goggles but with the opposite eye.

After putting on one set of goggles, look at a distant object through the extreme corner of one eye for about one minute. Do not read anything since this accentuates activity in the left brain. After a minute, evaluate your mood during this process. Then put on the other goggles, repeat the process, and compare your mood to your previous experience.

To state the mechanics of the brain simply, it is activity on the left side of your brain that is most indicative of feeling good particularly in people suffering from depression. It is activity on the left side of the brain that shortens or extinguishes negative feelings (Post Traumatic Stress disorder may be the left brain trying to keep a memory alive, rather than turning it off).

In people suffering from depression, modern imaging techniques have shown that the left area of the brain is less active than in people who do not suffer from depression. Antidepressant drugs seem to increase activity in this part of the brain.

Understanding these mechanics of the brain helps us to understand why certain activities tend to make us feel better. For instance, have you ever noticed how after talking about a problem you feel better, even though nothing may have changed? Talking is a left brain activity, and is important in building a positive mood.

Study and Discuss

Read Genesis 2:18

Is it good for us to be alone?

Read Psalm 32:3-6 and 39:2-3

How does silence affect the body and the spirit?

Read Isaiah 38:18-19

Why is life better than death?

Silence is not good for the human spirit. God designed into us a need and desire to be with people, to interact with others and live lives of praise to God. However, in depression we often adopt behaviors that are bad for our spirit.

Talking is critical to emotional and spiritual well being, but when people are sinking into depression, they often do less talking. Depression is frequently accompanied by social withdrawal and less conversational interaction with those around us. This change in behavior strengthens the grip that depression has on the mind.

While talking may not change anything about a certain situation, it helps to change the way your brain is processing information. As we talk to people around us, many things can happen. First of all, the focus of our attention is changed. Rather than dwelling on our misery, we have to focus on the person we are talking to.

When we talk about our problems with others, those individuals may help us to perceive our problems differently than we are perceiving them. They challenge us to adopt, or at least consider, other perspectives. Even if the person we are talking with merely listens to us, without offering any advice, the simple act of talking out a problem can change the way we feel about it.

When we talk about issues that have emotional content, we must translate feelings into objective words that someone else can understand. We don't just share feelings. We explain why we feel a certain way and how we think our life will be affected by the issues that trouble us. As we carry out this process, our minds are forced to think less emotionally and more logically by the mere act of communication.

In depression, emotions excessively color the interpretation of life in a way that does not necessarily reflect reality. The simple task of talking and interacting with others forces our brain to behave less emotionally and more objectively. Actively communicating with others is predominately a left brain activity.

The importance of communicating with others is highlighted by the fact that God constantly implores us to talk to him in prayer. One of the regular questions I receive as a minister is, *"If God already knows our hearts and our needs, why do we have to pray?"*

God doesn't need our prayers. God does know what we need before we ask for it (see Mt 6:8). The Bible tells us that God (Mt 5:45) *"causes his sun to rise on the evil and the good, and sends rain on the righteous and the unrighteous."*

Prayer is not an obligation we owe to God, but a gift he has given to us. In the act of prayer, our attention is shifted from how the world looks at problems and our focus becomes more spiritual. Of course, how much we know about the God to whom we are speaking, has a great deal to do with how this act changes our perspective. Nonetheless, I am constantly amazed by the number of Christians facing significant issues in life who simply do not employ this tool for problem solving.

Many times people have come to me for counseling regarding a wide range of problems that seem to have no good answer. Yet, when asked a simple questions such as, *"What do you think God would want you to do?"* or *"What resources has God given us to deal with this problem?"* these individuals quickly arrive at an appropriate solution.

In many instances the solutions to these problems were known in advance of our visit. The real issue was reluctance to carry out God's solution or to trust that God would ultimately provide the resources to manage the challenges these individuals faced. Many times, however, the solution discovered through this process represented a totally different way of thinking. These individuals may have talked about this issue with family, friends, and co-workers, but they had not seriously talked about this issue with God. God's perspective, though stored somewhere in our memories or easily determined once we put ourselves into a spiritual framework, had simply never been sought in prayer.

God designed us to actively communicate with others, including himself. It is not good for our body, mind, or spirit to withdraw into ourselves and stop communicating. If we conceive of the various parts of the brain as a muscle, the less we use certain parts of the brain the weaker they will become. The more we use certain parts of the brain, the stronger they will become. Modern brain scanning actually shows that depression changes the size of certain portions of the brain.

In depression, a portion of the brain called the hippocampus tends to shrink. In a recent study using PET brain scans, a particular form of talk therapy called "cognitive behavioral therapy" (CBT) helped this area of the brain to grow.[43] However, talk therapy changes the brain in a different way than do antidepressant drugs.

In the study just mentioned, equally depressed people were given PET brain scans before and after treatment using different therapies. One group received an antidepressant called "Paxil," and another group received CBT. While both groups experienced similar improvement in symptoms, their brain scans differed remarkably. Cognitive therapy increased activity in the hippocampus while Paxil increased activity in the frontal cortex.

The fact that antidepressants and therapy work on different areas of the brain, is one reason why combined therapies are far more effective and long lasting than one therapy alone. Antidepressants seem to help the brain dampen negative feelings, but talk therapy changes the strategy our brains use for interpreting and dealing with the world we encounter. Running the risk of over-simplification, drugs help us to turn down the volume on our negative feelings, cognitive therapy keeps negative feelings from getting started, and helps us stop them when they do.

What Other Activities Change Mood?

There are many other lifestyle changes that can positively shape our mood. Music is one of those universally recognized tools for changing our mood. Recently, brain scans have revealed how music not only changes our brains, but has different effects depending upon the particular brain that is listening to it.

People who have little or no music training, listen to music with primarily their right brains. When musicians listen to music, they show a great deal of activity on the left side of their brain.[44] While there is no study to confirm this, playing an instrument or singing will probably improve your mood more than listening to music.

---

[43]K. Goldapple, Z. Segal, C. Garson, M. Lau, P. Bieling, S. Kennedy, H. Mayberg, "Modulation of Cortical-Limbic Pathways in Major Depression ~ Treatment-Specific Effects of Cognitive Behavior Therapy" (Archives of General Psychiatry; 2004;61:34-41)

[44]Ohnishi, T. et al., (2001) "Functional Anatomy of musical perception in musicians" (Cerebral Cortex, 11:754 - 760)

The type of music we listen to also plays a role in shaping our mood. If you are depressed, listening to a tragic country music song or some angry and screaming heavy metal is probably not going to improve your disposition. Remember that in depression the music you "feel" like listening to, will tend toward supporting your present mood rather than lifting you out of it. "Misery loves company!"

When it comes to selecting music to play or music to listen to, you should follow the advice of the song by Jessie Matthews from Rogers and Hammerstein's musical "The King and I."

Whenever I feel afraid ~ I hold my head erect ~ And whistle a happy tune ~ So no one will suspect I'm afraid

While shivering in my shoes ~ I strike a careless pose ~ And whistle a happy tune ~ And no one ever knows I'm afraid

The result of this deception is very strange to tell

For when I fool the people I fear I fool myself as well

I whistle a happy tune ~ and every single time ~ The happiness in the tune ~ Convinces me that I'm not afraid

Spend less time watching T.V., particularly the news. There are two reasons for this. First of all, news tends toward the negative and sensational, rather than the positive and normal. If you are struggling to find positive thoughts then the news is not for you. However, if you must have news, read it in a newspaper or on the internet. Though the news may be the same, your brain will process it differently.

Television is particularly harmful for the depressed mind because of the way your brain processes information. Positive thoughts are more of a left side brain activity, but television virtually switches off the left side of your brain.[45] Watching television is predominantly a right brain activity that involves very little critical thinking. Reading, on the other hand, is more of a left brain activity. The more you can read or listen to information you must have, and the less you get it from T.V., the better you will feel.

You should also be selective in what type of material you choose to read or focus on. Spend more time reading in the Scriptures or other

---

[45]Krugman, Herbert E. (1971) "Brain wave Measures of Media Involvement" (Journal of Advertising Research 11.1: 3-9)

positive, mood enhancing, literature. As a general rule, the more you challenge your mind to grow through reading, watching, or listening, the better you will feel.

In depression, portions of the brain are literally shrinking. "Mind-expanding activities" is more than a mere expression. Your brain literally grows new connections as it learns. Avoid mind numbing activities. Seek out activities which challenge you to think, especially those activities which help you to think from God's point of view!

Lesson 3 ~ Weekly Activities

There is a great deal of information from this lesson that you need to implement into your life style. Wait at least a week before you continue with the next lesson and spend some time incorporating what you have learned through the activities below.

Within one or two days schedule a time to sit down with your family and discuss bed time, the amount of television you watch, and other habits and customs with your entire family. (WAKE THEM IN THE MIDDLE OF THE NIGHT IF NECESSARY TO HAVE THIS DISCUSSION!!!). If you live by yourself, schedule a time with your support partner, a family member or close friend, to discuss these issues so that you may receive some outside input.

It may be helpful to read out loud the section from this study on sleep and other activities to the people you are meeting with. You may want to encourage family members to read all or parts of this study that you feel are important.

The primary goal of this meeting is to discuss sleep patterns, television habits, and especially the amount of time you spend talking with others. Achieving a good sleep pattern may involve many other changes in your daily schedule. At this meeting you may want to discuss the necessity of making other significant changes in life style that will reduce stress and increase healthy and positive living patterns (such as adding music to the home environment, reading time, etc.).

On the line below write down the time and place when you would like to have such a meeting.

Life Style Discussion Time and Place

____

Write down some of the life style issues that you think need to be modified based upon what you read in this lesson.

____

____

____

____

____

Identifying Uppers and Downers

In Lesson 1 we briefly discussed activities that tend to lift our spirits, and activities that tend to depress our spirits. For instance, taking a walk or reading a book might be an activity that tends to lift you up, while watching T.V. or taking a nap may tend to bring you down.

As outlined in this lesson, different parts of our brain are engaged by different activities. This lesson showed that depression seeks to reinforce itself. In other words, our natural inclination when we are depressed, is to seek activities that will further our depression, rather than lift us out of it.

During the course of the next two weeks you should begin to identify, on a daily basis, your "Upper Activities" and your "Downer Activities." The central question in identifying these activities is not whether you feel like doing them at any given time, but rather how your mood is changed after or while you are doing them.

On a daily basis carefully examine your activities. In the Appendix at the back of this book on page A9 will find a sample method of tracking these activities. Over the next two weeks, utilize pages A10 - A13 to identify your unique uppers and downers.

Make log entries on a daily basis. Then use this information to alter your life style choices. When you feel like you are becoming depressed, try to choose activities that fall in your upper list. Avoid, as best you can, activities in your downer list.

Obviously, not all "downers" are avoidable. For instance, if your place of work is very stressful, you cannot simply quit your job (at least, not right away). However, even within a stressful workplace you may be able to reschedule activities to make it less stressful.

When examining your activities at work, try to schedule your most stressful activities for the time in the day when you have your highest energy, usually earlier in the day. Schedule your most enjoyable activities, or least stressful activities, for later in the day when you have low energy.

Although you will accomplish the same amount of work, your last memory of the day will be far more positive. Also, you will be more productive when handling the more stressful parts of your work because they have been scheduled for the times when you are best equipped to accomplish them.

Caring for the Body and Spirit God Gave me

Continue calling your support partner at least once a week. Make sure to log your progress in caring for your body and spirit on the sheets provided in the **Appendix**. Particularly focus on your sleep patterns and changes you are making to your daily routine.

Scripture Reading

Just like food for the stomach, regular Scripture reading provides nourishment for our spirits and should be done on a daily basis. These particular selections illustrate the importance of interaction with God and others in the Christian's life. At a minimum, you should read these selections during the course of this week and answer the questions for each reading.

For daily, or additional reading, you are encouraged to read the 1st and 2nd Epistles of John (not the Gospel, but 1st John near the back of the Bible). Consider reading a chapter or more a day from these Epistles.

Day 2 ~ Read 1 Corinthians 12:4-27

Did God make us all the same or different?

According to verse 7, why do we have different gifts?

Can we get along without each other?

Why should we strive to be in relationships with other people?

Day 4 ~ Read 2 Corinthians 1:1-11

When Paul receives comfort in his troubles, how does he make use of the comfort he has received?

Does Paul see his distresses and troubles as something that isolates him from other people?

Why do you think Paul likes to share both his troubles and victories with others?

DAY 6 ~ Read Psalm 116

Why is it important to share our concerns with God in prayer?

Will the Lord abandon us?

- NOTES -

- NOTES -

Lesson 4

Thinking Styles and Their Effects on the Brain

What's The Point? *From infancy on we learn "thinking styles" for interpreting our world. These styles physically alter our brain and our brain chemistry. In this lesson we become acquainted with harmful thinking styles and the techniques and resources for changing them.*

How Do Thoughts Change Our Brain?

At the present most people believe that depression is "caused" by a chemical imbalance in the brain. In previous lessons we have introduced modern research that shows that these chemical imbalances and other aspects of brain structure can be altered by our diet, exercise, our thoughts and even our social activities. The cause and effect relationship of depression and anxiety to our brain chemistry and structure is not nearly as clear cut as most people presume.

Our thoughts and activities can either contribute to depression or help lift us out of depression. In particular, stress hormones that are produced as a result of mental stress, are a major contributing factor to depression and anxiety.[46]

In this and subsequent lessons we will identify thinking patterns that contribute to stress, anxiety, and depression. It is important to understand that without identifying and changing our thinking patterns, the downward cycle of depression cannot be stopped. Chemical imbalances may exist in our brains, but they exist in a cyclical relationship to our thoughts. How we think can cause these imbalances, and these imbalances then influence how we think.

As discussed in earlier lessons, modern clinical research has confirmed that psychotherapy alone is about as effective in improving depression symptoms as placing a patient on antidepressants (55% vs.

---

[46]Adelson, Rachel, "Hard-hitting hormones: The stress-depression link", (Monitor on Psychology, January, 2005 Vol 36:1, p. 24)

52%).[47] One might reasonably ask, "If this is the case, why doesn't everyone use psychotherapy?" There are several reasons for this, but the two most significant are COST and TIME!

The cost of psychotherapy varies throughout the nation, but in 2002 the average cost per session was about $100. A typical patient may need 15 to 20 sessions, costing from $1,500 to $2,000, to get the same kind of initial improvement provided by antidepressant medication, which generally costs $1,000 per year .[48]

Since both therapies yield similar initial results, which course of action would you encourage as an insurance company, or which would you prefer to pay out of your own pocket? Also, if time is precious to you, which would you rather do? Take a pill per day, or take time off from work, travel to a therapist's office, spend an hour, get back to work, and also do some reading and mental exercises during the week?

In a world where money and time are precious commodities, the choice seems obvious. Take the pill! The problem with this approach is that the easy solution doesn't last. People treated with antidepressant drugs alone have a relapse rate approaching 80%.

Recent studies show that while psychotherapy alone and medication alone have similar initial results, psychotherapy alone has a lower relapse rate.[49] Several studies have shown that when medication and psychotherapy are combined, the relapse rate drops from the 75%-80% range into the 25% -35% range. The cost of such combination therapy, however, is very high in terms of dollars and time.

Despite these costs, recent evidence is overwhelming that the positive effect of added psychotherapy to drug therapy is not an accident. Psychotherapy attacks depression in a totally different manner than

---

[47]Keller, Martin B., and others, "A Comparison of Nefazodone, the Cognitive Behavioral-Analysis System of Psychotherapy, and Their Combination for the Treatment of Chronic Depression" (The New England Journal of Medicine 2000 342:1462-1470, 1518-1520)

[48]http://www.healthyplace.com/Communities/depression/news/antidepressants_vs_therapy.asp, © 2000-2004 HealthyPlace.com, Inc

[49]Kuipers, E., Garety, P., Fowler, D., et al, "East Anglia randomized controlled trial of cognitive - behavioural therapy for psychosis" (British Journal of Psychiatry, 1997, Vol. 171 p. 328-33)

antidepressant therapy. The key seems to be an area of the brain called the midline frontal lobe.

When a healthy person encounters new information, a critical question that must be answered is the relationship of that stimulus to yourself. Does the information you receive need to be processed emotionally, or logically? Will the information bring you reward, punishment, or should it just be ignored? For most of the information we receive from the outside world, the process of making this decision begins in an area of the brain called the "Thalamus."

With the exception of smell, the thalamus pre-processes all of the information your brain receives from the outside world. The thalamus has three circuits running through its walnut sized core. One circuit (called the Specific Relay Nuclei) is constantly scanning the cerebral cortex looking for neurons that are active.

When this circuit receives input, the thalamus then goes to a reference circuit where it compares the input being received to a database of information that has been recognized in the past. After comparing new input to previous information, this second circuit (called the Reticular Formation) makes intelligent guesses about what is being seen, heard, or felt. On rare occasions, when the thalamus finds no answer, it tells the mind that it is mistaken and that nothing has been seen, heard or felt.

The third circuit in the thalamus (called the Intralaminar) is constantly searching memory to see what associations might be made with the sensory input that has just been identified. Thus, if we are seeing the Eiffel tower (or a picture of it), the third circuit will likely pick up pieces of memory about Paris, or France, or towers in general.

The thalamus doesn't decide exactly what information you are receiving, it just makes a best guess, creating a bias, and then sends the information along for additional processing. The information goes in two directions. Along one path the information is processed emotionally, along another path the information is processed logically.

Think of the thalamus as a business secretary sorting mail. In the mail sorting process a secretary must decide, based on very incomplete information, how an organization will process information it receives from its customers. If the letter is only addressed to the business, the secretary calls upon his or her memory of how the mail was handled in the past, or the memory of the business or individual sending the mail, to make this sorting decision.

A new secretary usually makes a lot of mistakes in sorting mail. The lack of experience prevents the secretary from making proper decisions, and also lengthens the sorting process. However, while experience may speed the process and lead to better decision making, experience in mail sorting can also be a liability.

Changes in policy or staff may mean mail must be directed differently. However, in making quick sorting decisions, these new procedures may be forgotten, and old habits will exert themselves. This will be particularly true if the secretary is over stressed.

Too much familiarity may lead the experienced secretary to overlook obvious details that a new secretary would notice. For example, mail from a business normally directed to John Doe is specifically addressed to Jane Doe. However, the experienced secretary doesn't look carefully at addresses. Since all information from this company was previously sent to John Doe it goes into John Doe's mail bin. A new secretary would be far less likely to make this mistake.

When information comes into the brain, the thalamus makes a quick decision as to the meaning of the information. It then sends the information down two separate paths to be analyzed for emotional content and a more reasoned, logical response.[50] Whether this initial analysis is accurate or not, it will set the tone for our initial response to the information. Our emotional processing circuit is particularly vulnerable to this initial bias.

Our emotional response to situations is faster than our logical response, by about a half second, because it involves a shorter circuitry path. If someone throws a hard object at you from 42 feet away at 90 miles an hour, you want that kind of thinking speed. You don't have a lot of time to evaluate whether or not the object is going to hit you. The natural response to this kind of event is fear. In the blink of an eye the normal person will dive out of the way in response to this visual information.

---

[50]Restak, pp. 115-116

The problem with this automatic and rapid fear response is that if you're a professional baseball player, you will never hit a fastball lying on the ground. If this response system could not be altered, there would be no professional baseball.

A part of the brain called the "Amygdala" is responsible for emotional processing and triggering the fight/flight response. After the thalamus makes its initial assessment, the amygdala processes that information and initiates a reaction before reason ever gets into gear. You literally act before you think. These emotional reactions affect how our reason will interpret the information, and how the information from this event will be stored into memory and accessed in the future.

We all have experienced this process at work. We meet someone new and instantly don't like that person, but we can't explain why. We walk into a room and we sense something is wrong, but we can't consciously explain what makes us feel that way. Sometimes our emotions guess right, but particularly in depression they show a propensity to guess wrong, and as depression grows we find it increasingly difficult to shut our negative emotions off.

The reason circuit can shut down the fear response. The reason circuit runs through the cortex and the hippocampus. The hippocampus is largely responsible for storing new conscious memories and connecting related memories.

To illustrate how these two circuits work together, imagine yourself walking through a forest, and off to the side you see something dark and curled up next to the path. If you were a child who grew up in the inner city and had never seen a snake you probably wouldn't react at all. Your thalamus might identify the object as trash, and you would just keep on walking. If you grew up in the western states and had once been bitten by a rattle snake, you might jump out of your shoes and start running.

As it turns out, the object was just an old rubber hose that some environmentally unconscious individual had discarded along the path. Upon close inspection the hose looked nothing like a snake, but the information your amygdala used as it initiated the fear response was not based on complete information.

While your emotional response was irrational, the intensity of that response set the agenda for at least several seconds of thinking. If you were sufficiently frightened, you might never return to that path. Even if you did realize the object was an old hose, you might still feel anxious for several minutes.

The hippocampus provides a wider context for information through the access of memory, and enables us to store new conscious memories. People with damage to the hippocampus can remember events from the distant past and from the day in which they are living, but cannot recall yesterday or any other event after the hippocampus was damaged. Despite this inability to store conscious memories, people with a damaged hippocampus can still learn new motor skills, and learn new emotional reactions.

The amygdala seems to have a distinct memory system, or memory access system. This system lies below the level of consciousness. For example, if an individual with a damaged hippocampus is frightened when walking into a room in a previous experience, they will become tense and anxious when approaching that room the next day, but will not be able to explain the reason for their anxiety.

In a healthy individual, the information sent through the thalamus ~ cortex ~ hippocampus pathway, eventually gets back to the amygdala. In the earlier illustration, once the logic circuit recognizes the hose, it sends a signal to the amygdala essentially telling it to chill out. The next question for the brain is, "What should I do with this experience?"

You might just laugh at yourself, and continue on your walk. You could start looking at the trees again and do some day dreaming. If you direct your mind elsewhere, chances are when you walk down the path again, you will pay less attention both emotionally and logically to the old hose as you pass it.

After several walks you will eventually reach the point where your brain does not react at all to the presence of the hose. The thalamus will still receive the same sensory input it had on your first walk, but both your emotion and reason circuits will essentially decide that this object is not worth thinking about.

A different mental approach might be chosen if you were once bitten by a snake. After calming down from your initial reaction, you could go back to that traumatic event in life and rehearse every moment again in your mind. Though you didn't die, just thinking about that possibility may cause your mind to jump to other tragic events.

You might start thinking about the death of a dear friend or close relative. The remainder of your walk is filled with a rehearsal of dark and intense memories. The next day you may happily begin another walk, but as you pass the spot where the hose is located your thoughts drift in a negative direction.

Consciously you are not startled or afraid of the hose. You didn't make a conscious decision to start thinking about negative events. In fact, no specific negative memories may even enter into your consciousness. Yet, as you pass that old hose you start to feel sad or anxious. The intensity of the experience on the previous day, coupled with persistent negative thoughts, created a new trigger for negative emotional memories.

Do we have any control over this process? If we couldn't control this process, there would be no professional baseball. If you take the average person off the street, put him in a batter's box, and let him see for the first time what a professional fastball looks like up close, no reassurance from the pitcher will keep that person from flinching. However, through conscious effort, practice, and experience, the professional baseball player can learn to stay in the batter box and swing at the 90 miles per hour fast ball, rather than ducking.

Recent studies of brain scans have discovered that people who currently suffer from depression, or people who suffered from depression in the past but are not currently receiving treatment, have a hyperactive emotional circuit. The negative emotional switch is turned on, even when conscious thought is directed elsewhere.

One study compared the brain scans of healthy patients, depressed patients, and patients who have recovered from depression after they were exposed to an emotionally sad stimulus.[51] The study found that a particular area of the brain, the "midline frontal lobe" showed decreased activity in depressed patients and people who have recovered from depression, but remained active in healthy patients.

---

[51]Liotti,M; Mayberg, H. , et. al, "Unmasking Disease-Specific Cerebral Blood Flow Abnormalities: Mood Challenge in Patients With Remitted Unipolar Depression" (American Journal of Psychiatry 2002 159: 1830-1840)

This midline frontal area of the brain is part of the reason circuit. It essentially shuts down your emotions at an appropriate time and allows you to move on with your life. You may have been sad, but you don't dwell on it. You may have been anxious, but now you are calm. A single event doesn't ruin your entire day. Emotions are essentially turned off as your attention is directed elsewhere. At least, that is how the brain is supposed to work.

In depression or anxiety this mechanism for shutting down sadness or anxious thoughts does not work properly. Life and activity move forward. Conscious attention may be shifted, but the emotional part of the brain is stuck in the on position. Even during happy events or calm events, sadness or anxiety are experienced.

It seems that antidepressant drugs have their effect by working on the areas of the brain which produce our negative feelings. In other words, these drugs dampen our emotional circuitry. Some people refer to the way that antidepressant drugs work as a "bottom up approach."

Antidepressant drug therapy alters the brain chemistry in the bottom or "limbic" region of the brain that drives emotions.[52] These drugs decrease your emotional response to stimulation. The problem is that antidepressants don't limit their effects to negative thoughts.

Loss of sexual desire is a frequent side effect of antidepressants. People on antidepressants often complain that they have become zombies or are emotionless. While there is less sadness, there is also less joy. The deep holes of depression are not so deep, but the emotional highs of life are not so high either. Life is a little more bland.

By contrast, a particular form of therapy called "Cognitive Behavior Therapy" (CBT) changes how people deal with sad thoughts. Some people refer to this as a "top down approach." Brain scans reveal that people who receive CBT show increased activity in the midline frontal lobe. This increased brain activity approaches the type of activity that is seen in people who have never been depressed.

Whereas drugs dampen emotions, CBT helps you learn a better strategy for when to turn the negative emotion switch on, and a more

---

[52]Goldapple, K.; and others, "Modulation of Cortical-Limbic Pathways in Major Depression ~ Treatment-Specific Effects of Cognitive Behavior Therapy" (Archives of General Psychiatry. 2004;61:34-41)

effective way to turn it off. The pioneer in cognitive behavioral therapy is an American psychologist named Aaron T. Beck.

Perhaps oversimplified, Beck assumed that the depressed person interprets events incorrectly, always assuming the negative. The thoughts are plausible and may be thoughts normal individuals could have, but when piled up on top of each other they create a weight of depressed thoughts, a downward spiral into a black hole of negativity from which the person is unable to emerge.

By identifying flaws in our reasoning process, and then building new ways of interpreting life, cognitive therapy addresses the causes of depression and produces far more lasting results. To understand how cognitive therapy works the following illustration is provided.

Answer Privately Then Discuss

Imagine this scenario: ***You are walking down the street and see some friends. You wave at them, but they don't wave back.***

1) **What are the possible explanations for the people not waving back?**

2) **Putting the "best construction" on everything, of the above possibilities which would you pick?**

3) **Using the "worst case scenario," which of the above possibilities would you pick?**

CBT presumes that the path to depression begins when people have an overall tendency to presume the "worst case scenario" rather than the best case scenario. As depression deepens, the "best construction" answers may not even enter the individual's mind. In the extremely depressed, there is no choice between "they didn't see me!" and "they are mad at me!" The former thought never occurs. Even if those same friends were friendly at the next encounter, the depressed person will assume that they are just pretending to be friendly.

Further evidence that depression is linked to a diminished use of logic in the reasoning process is offered in a study by Aaron Beck and David Braff.[53] Depressed individuals were asked to interpret abstract concepts that were presented to them such as those contained in proverbs and sayings. When compared to individuals who were not depressed, people suffering from depression demonstrated a greater difficulty interpreting the meaning of phrases such as "a stitch in time saves nine."

The mind which is being driven primarily by negative emotion will be under constant stress. This stress will eventually cause physical damage to the brain and will negatively impact the entire body. Excessive stress hormones cause the hippocampus to shrink, thereby further diminishing the brain's ability to turn off negative emotions. While drugs may offer temporary mood improvement, without a fundamental change in how the brain interprets events, depression will ultimately reoccur.

The positive role of CBT in treating depression does not imply that drugs have no value. By turning down the volume on the emotional speaker system, drugs may enhance someone's ability to do the hard mental labor required in CBT. People in very deep depression may need this boost. However, drugs alone do nothing to change the thinking patterns that drive you in the direction of depression. This explains both the high relapse rate for people on antidepressant medication alone, as well as the delayed reaction of antidepressants.

When people begin taking an antidepressant, serotonin levels increase rather quickly. Yet, it is usually three to four weeks before there is a noticeable difference in symptoms. If depression were indeed a mere chemical imbalance, this should not be the case.

Several studies, based on brain imaging, have shown that people receiving antidepressant drug therapy do not begin to experience relief

---

[53]Braff, D. L.; Beck, A. T.; "Thinking disorder in depression" (Archives of General Psychiatry, 1974 vol 31: pp. 456-459)

of their symptoms until the hippocampus begins to grow.[54] However, when compared with cognitive therapy, the hippocampus is the area of the brain least effected by antidepressant therapy alone, and most profoundly affected by cognitive therapy. This fact dramatically demonstrates why the two therapies should be used in combination.

While changing how the brain thinks is possible, it is not easy. Like a stroke victim who must train new parts of the brain to take over tasks once performed by other parts of the brain, people involved in cognitive therapy must work hard and practice certain tasks to rewire their thought processes.

How Does Our Brain Program its Thoughts?

Thoughts are not simply random events in our brain, nor are they entirely dictated by events around us. Thoughts are complex associations which involve input from all our senses and our memory, including our emotional memory.

In a fascinating experiment, a researcher named Gordon Bower put students in a particular mood by listening to happy or sad music. He then asked the students to memorize 16 different words. The next day he invited the students back and again put them in a particular mood. Half the students were placed in the same mood they experienced the previous day (happy or sad), and half the students were placed in the opposite mood. All the students were then asked to remember the words they had memorized.[55]

Students who were placed in the same mood, either happy or sad, had a relatively equal ability to recall the words they had memorized. Students who were placed in the opposite mood had much more difficulty remembering the words they had memorized.

In another experiment students were again placed in a happy or sad mood, and then asked to recall events from the last two weeks of their

---

[54] Rosack, Jim, "Antidepressants May Prevent Hippocampus From Shrinking" (Psychiatric News September 5, 2003 Volume 38:17 p. 24)

[55] Eich, E., & Metcalfe, J. (1989). "Mood dependent memory for internal versus external events." (Journal of Experimental Psychology: Learning, Memory and Cognition vol 15:443-455)

lives. Students placed in a happy mood recalled primarily happy events, whereas students in a sad mood recalled primarily sad events.[56] Clinical psychologists have often noted that patients suffering from depression often describe their childhood negatively while in depression, but far more positively after depression has passed.

Emotion changes what we can remember from the past and what we learn from the present. In another experiment students were placed in specific moods under hypnosis and given descriptions of 36 different events to remember. Some events were sad, some were happy, and others described anger. Equal time was given to study each event.

When brought out of hypnosis, the students were asked to recall as many events as possible. Students placed in a happy mood were able to remember happy events better than other events. Students placed in a sad mood could remember more sad events, and those placed in an angry mood were better able to remember angry events. In this study it was not the current mood that interfered with recall. Rather, the mood while learning dramatically changed the ability of the brain to retain and recall new information.[57]

While different areas of the brain focus on special activities, they also are constantly interacting with each other. Reading the word bird stimulates the language centers of our brain to recall the meaning of the word. The visual centers of the brain may be stimulated to recall various images of birds. The emotional centers of the brain may be stimulated to recall the good feelings of a recent camping trip, or the sad feelings of a pet bird that just died. If you have a pet bird or hunt birds, the word may even stimulate the smell center.

All of these interactions take place in the blink of an eye without conscious effort. While we may not consciously focus our attention on all of these different associations, they are still taking place. Sometimes these associations have crippling effects on the lives of people.

---

[56]Snyder, M., & White, P. (1982). "Moods and memories: elation, depression, and the remembering of the events of one's life" (Journal of Personality vol 50:149-167)

[57]Gilligan, S. G. (1982). "Mood intensity and learning of congruous material" (Ph.D. thesis, Stanford Psychology Department, Stanford University)

A phobia is an extreme and irrational reaction to a specific stimulus. Fear of spiders, mice, flying, heights and close places are just a few of the phobias people may have. Rational, logical, left brain type thinking is not active when people are confronted with their particular phobic stimulus. The image of the spider, for instance provokes such an intense fear response that no amount of reasoned thinking can convince the amygdala to chill out. Phobias cannot simply be wished away. Overcoming a phobia requires a conscious effort to retrain the thinking mechanisms of the brain.

One of the more effective techniques for eliminating phobias is called desensitization or exposure therapy, a form of cognitive therapy. In more traditional psychology the focus would be to try and understand where the phobia came from (a childhood experience or tragic event). In CBT the origin of a phobia is relatively unimportant. The simple fact is that the visual stimulus of a spider is hard wired to the brain's emotional center for fear. This link must be broken and a new thought path must be created.

In desensitization or exposure therapy, a person is slowly and methodically brought into closer contact with whatever frightens them. Relaxation and breathing exercises may be used to help reduce anxiety symptoms. Other environmental stimuli that tend to make the person feel safe and secure (pleasing aromas, music), may be introduced to help build new mental associations.

After repeated exposure the person becomes more accustomed to, and feels safer with, the anxiety producing stimulus. A somewhat interesting side effect of this type of therapy is that those individuals who begin with fears of specific animals, often end up purchasing spiders, mice, etc. as pets.

Like a stroke victim laying down new mental pathways to control body movement, people suffering from crippling mental conditions, such as depression and phobias, need to lay down new mental paths to interpret the world around them. This can be very difficult because certain associations have become, over time, automatic.

These automatic associations may shut down altogether our logical thought processing. Thus, brain scans of people suffering from depression and anxiety, show decreased activity in the higher reasoning parts of the brain. The hippocampus, an important part of our learning circuit, literally shrinks. Changing these mental processes cannot be accomplished by short term effort. Rewiring the brain requires concentrated and repeated effort.

Not all neural connections in the brain are equal. When memories and thought processes are being formed, neurons actually grow and strengthen connections with other neurons. Repeating an event makes these connections stronger to the point where they become automatic.

In obsessive compulsive disorder these connections can become so strong that people lose the ability to shut them off. Intense therapy or drug intervention can help the individual learn how to turn off these mental connections, but in rare instances obsessive compulsive behavior can only be cured surgically. Surgeons literally sever the neural connections involved in a particular thought process to stop the compulsive behavior.

Strong neural connections are not always bad. Athletes and musicians train themselves so that they no longer have to think about performing certain tasks. The task becomes automatic. Sometimes responses can become so automatic that people lose the ability to describe the response without repeating the behavior.

Cashiers have to remember different entry codes and numbers. Pausing for each customer to look up a special code is tedious, so the cashier makes an effort to memorize them. Speaking a number out loud is often an aid to the memorization process. In time the cashier becomes so familiar with the special codes that there is no conscious act to recall the relationship between the item and code. As the item appears on the counter, the cashier's fingers automatically enter the special code into the cash register.

One day a neighboring cashier who is new at the job calls out "What's the code for bananas?" The experienced cashier can type the numbers without thinking, but has not uttered them out loud for months. At least twenty times earlier in the day the numbers were typed, but no amount of mental effort can recall the audible memory of these numbers. Unable to answer the question, the frustrated cashier places her fingers on her own register and watches her fingers as they effortlessly glide to the appropriate numbers. Only by watching her fingers can she tell the new cashier what numbers to use.

When first learning these numbers, they were associated with verbal cues. In time, these numbers became more closely connected to the physical cues of moving fingers. The verbal cues once associated with the numbers were lost. Concentrated verbal effort was replaced by an automatic physical response.

In depression and anxiety there are certain automatic responses that take place which help to perpetuate a state of sadness or anxiousness. These responses are learned ways of interpreting life and relationships. Frequently these mental relationships are formed at an early age.

As depression deepens (or anxiety rises) the mental processes are repeated so often and become so automatic that we lose the ability to see the world in an alternate way. Breaking this cycle involves identifying the faulty methods of thinking we use and training ourselves to use new thinking styles. At first, these changes require concentrated and repeated effort, but in time they can become more automatic and effortless.

How Does Cognitive Therapy Change the Mind?

Beck has identified certain destructive thinking styles that are characteristic of many mood disorders, but particularly depression and anxiety. Cognitive therapy trains people to recognize these thinking styles as destructive, and encourages the use of more constructive thinking patterns.

Cognitive therapy is hard work, similar to the effort that stroke victims must employ to retrain their brains. It involves the memorization of certain concepts, practice in identifying when you are using certain thinking styles, and then practicing new alternatives to problem solving and interpreting life events. In "Gospel Therapy" spiritual principles are added to the traditional CBT model. In many cases, spiritual principles replace and even contradict some of the coping skills that would be used in standard CBT training.

For the purposes of introducing you to cognitive therapy the following list is offered. This list details commonly agreed upon thinking styles or "cognitive distortions" that are characteristic in people who are suffering from depression.[58]

It should be noted that occasionally everyone will make use of these thinking styles. What distinguishes clinical depression is the dominant influence of these thinking styles. For the clinically depressed individual these are not the occasional methods used for interpreting life. In clinical depression these thinking styles become the dominant, and sometimes exclusive, method for interpreting life.

1. **ALL-OR-NOTHING THINKING:** You see things in black-and-white categories. If your performance falls short of perfect, you see yourself as a total failure.
2. **OVER-GENERALIZATION:** You see a single negative event as a never-ending pattern of defeat.
3. **MENTAL FILTER:** You pick one negative detail and dwell on it exclusively so that your vision of all reality becomes darkened, like the drop of ink that discolors the entire beaker of water.
4. **DISQUALIFYING THE POSITIVE:** You reject positive experiences by insisting they "don't count" for some reason or other. In this way you can maintain a negative belief that is contradicted by your everyday experiences.
5. **JUMPING TO CONCLUSIONS:** You make a negative interpretation even though there are no definite facts that convincingly support your conclusion. This jumping to conclusions has two different forms.
   A. **MIND READING:** You arbitrarily conclude that someone is reacting negatively to you, and you don't bother to check this out.
   B. **NEGATIVE PREDICTION**: You can anticipate that things will turn out badly, and you feel convinced that your prediction is an already-established fact.
6. **MAGNIFICATION OR MINIMIZATION:** You exaggerate the importance of things (such as your goof-up or someone else's

---

[58]Burns, David D., "Feeling Good: The New Mood Therapy" (Avon Books, 1980, 1999 p. 42)

achievement), or you inappropriately shrink things until they appear tiny (your good qualities or the imperfections of others).

7. **EMOTIONAL REASONING:** You assume that your negative emotions necessarily reflect the way things really are: "I feel it, therefore it must be true."
8. **SHOULD STATEMENTS:** You try to motivate yourself with should and shouldn't, as if you had to be whipped and punished before you could be expected to do anything. "Musts" and "oughts" are also offenders. The emotional consequences are guilt. When you direct "should" statements toward others, you feel anger, frustration, and resentment.
9. **LABELING AND MISLABELING:** This is an extreme form of over-generalization. Instead of describing your error, you attach a negative label to yourself. "I'm a loser." When someone else's behavior rubs you the wrong way, you attach a negative label to him: "He's a louse!" Mislabeling involves describing an event with language that is highly colored and emotionally loaded.
10. **PERSONALIZATION**: You see yourself as the cause of some negative external event, which in fact you were not primarily responsible for.

In future lessons we will look more closely at each of these categories and identify the mental and spiritual tools necessary to combat them.

WHAT IS THE ROLE OF SPIRITUALITY IN DEPRESSION?

Read And Answer

Without discussion, write down an answer to the question, "Why should Christians not steal?" (This response will be used later in the lesson)

Cognitive therapy has proven effective in combating depression because it alters how the mind interprets events. Spirituality is a critical component in this interpretive process. Spirituality is a reference point for what is good and bad, the meaning and purpose of life, goals and values. Spirituality also differs in definition between individuals and religious systems.

Christianity is a unique spiritual system. Christianity is not simply a morality, but a wholly different view of the reality around us. Christian faith can be a powerful tool in overcoming depression, but only when we recognize and employ its central truth as the guiding principal for our lives.

Unfortunately, many Christians miss the real point of God's revelation to us in Christ. Faith is boiled down to moral codes and doctrinal formulations. Obedience and knowledge are emptied of the real substance of the Christian religion. That substance is found in God's grace as revealed in the message and work of Christ.

Christianity is fundamentally about God's promises and gifts, centered in God's forgiveness to us through the saving work of Jesus Christ. However, the word forgiveness does not exhaust the depth of God's grace to us in Christ. As one of my seminary professors once noted, the gospel is like a many faceted jewel that shines a little differently depending upon the angle from which you view it.

On your death bed the focus is resurrection. Certainly this hope is rooted in the forgiveness we have through Christ's redeeming work on the cross, but the main aspect of the gospel that addresses this life condition is the free gift of heaven. When someone is agonizing over adultery or some other sin, forgiveness is the primary aspect of the gospel that is focused on. Certainly this forgiveness enables us to join Christ in heaven, but the focus is on relieving guilt in the here and now.

Paul says, (2Co 1:20) *"For no matter how many promises God has made, they are 'Yes' in Christ. And so through him the 'Amen' is spoken by us to the glory of God."* In his letter to the Romans, speaking on the many aspects of God's grace, Paul writes:

> (Rm 8:31-32) *"What, then, shall we say in response to this? If God is for us, who can be against us? He who did not spare his own Son,*

but gave him up for us all--how will he not also, along with him, graciously give us all things?"

The essence of the Christian life is not rooted in moral codes but in the fullness of God's saving grace. The historic Christian creeds, such as the Apostles' or Nicene Creed, are all about what God has done for us and are virtually silent on man's response. Christian morality is not rooted in obedience but in trust. Christian morality is not a response to God's threats, nor something we owe God. Christian morality should be the "automatic" lifestyle for those who rightly understand what God has done and will do for us. We are saved by grace, and not by what we do.

Study and Discuss

What reasons did you write down earlier for not stealing?

Read Matthew 6:24-34 and Hebrews 13:5-6

What motive does God supply to us to prevent us from being tempted with money or material things?

Based on the verses above, how would you now respond to the question "Why should Christians not steal?"

Some of you may have been familiar with the verses quoted above. Possibly you have memorized portions of those verses. These particular verses of Scripture are centered in the grace and promises of God. Yet, the overwhelming majority of Christians (98% in my personal experience) when asked "Why should Christians not steal?" never reference these positive, gospel centered promises. Even though they may know these bible verses, their thoughts focus on negative ideas such as "It's wrong," "God forbids it," "It hurts other people" and the like.

The Christian faith is a powerful tool in combating depression, but the center of that faith *(which is the "Gospel" or "Good News" about Jesus)* does not come naturally nor automatically into our minds. While we may know the doctrinal formulations that make up this faith, and follow to the best of our ability its moral code, the real essence of this faith can often lie untapped in our mental processes.

Our automatic responses are shaped more by law than by gospel. Our fears, doubts and worries drive our behaviors and thoughts rather than God's grace and God's promises. Paradoxically, our prayers to God to seek his help will often begin, "Lord, what am I going to do?"

Christianity supplies to the cognitive process ideas which have no basis in the realities we observe. In helping a patient deal with death, a therapist, particularly one paid by the government, can only say it is part of the natural process of life. "All good things must come to end!" It is only through faith in God's revelation to us in Christ that death can be interpreted as a gateway to new life, and a glorious beginning.

The Apostle Paul once wrote, (1Co 15:19-20) *"If only for this life we have hope in Christ, we are to be pitied more than all men. But Christ has indeed been raised from the dead, the firstfruits of those who have fallen asleep."* The Christian's view of life runs through the filter of the promised life to come. Our values are shaped not by the pursuit of earthly treasures, but by the hope of (Mt 6:20) *"treasures in heaven, where moth and rust do not destroy, and where thieves do not break in and steal."*

Secular cognitive therapists do not have these tools of hope, love, grace, and forgiveness at their disposal. Spirituality, particularly Christian spirituality, adds a new dimension to cognitive training. Sometimes the Christian viewpoint merely supplements the standard training. In some cases, the Christian interpretive model will differ radically from the secular cognitive model. Finally, the Christian model fills in the spaces where the secular cognitive model has no positive way to deal with the often depressing facts of life.

Lesson 4 ~ Weekly Activities

This week we begin a more intense focus on matters of the mind and spirit. As we begin to change our focus, we cannot neglect the body. Remember that our relationship with God is as a whole person: body, mind and spirit. Neglecting any part of this triad can negatively impact the other parts.

Review Activities

Strong familiarity with the list of cognitive distortions will play an important role in upcoming lessons and your ability to change your thinking patterns. Read through and think about the list of distortions provided in Lesson 4 each day of this upcoming week. Check each day below when you have completed this activity.

☐ Monday ☐ Tuesday ☐ Wednesday ☐ Thursday

☐ Friday ☐ Saturday ☐ Sunday

Identifying Uppers and Downers

Continue to identify, on a daily basis, your "Upper Activities" and your "Downer Activities" as discussed in Lesson 3. The central question in identifying these activities is not whether you feel like doing them at any given time, but rather how your mood is changed after or while you are doing them. Write down your uppers or downers on the sheets designed for this activity contained in the **Appendix**.

Caring for the Body and Spirit God Gave me

If you have a support partner, continue to contact them at least once a week to talk about your progress. Make sure to write down on a daily basis your sleep, exercise, diet, and devotional achievements. For the rest of your lessons you will be given some specific devotional readings that support the concepts of each lesson.

It is recommended that you do these readings, and answer the associated questions, on day 2, day 4, and day 6 of this lesson cycle. However, each day should include some time in God's word. For the coming week you are encouraged to read 3-4 chapters each day in the

Gospel of Mark. By the end of the week you should have completed the entire Gospel.

Scripture Reading

Day 2 ~ Read 1 Kings 19:1-18

Why did Elijah want to die?

Did Elijah see himself as a success?

According to Elijah (see verse 19:10), was there any reason for him to continue to minister as a prophet?

According to God (see verse 19:18), was there any reason for him to continue to minister?

Do you think Elijah expected God to harshly judge the Israelites?

Why do you think God didn't appear in the wind, earthquake, or fire, but instead made himself known through a gentle whisper?

Day 4 ~ Read Background and then Job 19:19-29; 40:1-9; 42:1-17

Background: Job was a righteous man, but had been afflicted by many troubles. His friends, who supposedly came to comfort him, basically told him, *"Job, you must have done something pretty bad for all this to happen to you. Admit what you have done so that God will stop punishing you!"*

According to Job 19:19-29, does Job accept his friends interpretation of his troubles, or does he believe that God still cares for him and will deliver him?

According to Job 40:1-9, does it do any good to get angry with God and blame him for our troubles?

According to Job 42:1-17, Who was right about God? Job, or his friends?

What was the only thing God asked Job to do?

Besides praying that God would be merciful to his friends, what did God require of Job so that God would bless him and make him prosperous?

Day 6 ~ Read Matthew 6:24-34

What should not be the focus of our lives?

What should be the focus of our lives?

What promise does Jesus make that enables us to change our focus?

- NOTES -

Lesson 5
The Mental Distortions That Conflict With God's World View

What's the Point? *Our sinful human nature leads us to interpret the world in a distorted and negative way leading to depression. In this lesson we become more familiar with God's world view which is rooted in his grace and love for us. When we adopt God's method for interpreting life in this world, he will lead us to a more positive and productive life.*

How Does God View the World and Us?

Read Silently and Quickly Answer the Following

1) **Can you in some way speak of yourself as being perfect (Yes or No)?**

2) **Have you been baptized (Yes or No)?**

3) **For what reason or purpose did God send His Son Jesus to die on the cross?**

The word "Gospel" literally means "Good News." Look at the following Bible passages and write down a working definition of the gospel.

Study and Discuss

Read Romans 1:16-17; Acts 20:24 and 1 Corinthians 15:1-4

Write down a working definition of the gospel.

For many people, John 3:16 epitomizes the gospel:

(Jn 3:16-17) *"For God so loved the world that he gave his one and only Son, that whoever believes in him shall not perish but have eternal life. For God did not send his Son into the world to condemn the world, but to save the world through him."*

The gospel is good news. The gospel represents the promises God makes to us in Scripture. The gospel of God's grace in Jesus Christ should be the interpretive formula, the motive, for life in this world.

Study and Discuss

Read Romans 1:17

What principle should determine the righteous actions of Christians in this world?

Read Romans 6:14, Galatians 3:12 and 5:18

Should Christians live by God's law or by God's grace?

That which truly distinguishes a Christian action from the same moral act performed by a non-Christian is the motivation. The Bible says, (Heb 11:6) *"without faith it is impossible to please God."* Yet, in the decision making process, Christians rarely reference their faith in the gospel.

In the previous lesson we asked the question, *"Why should Christians not steal?"* The answer most people gave was something like "It's a sin," "It's wrong," "God will punish you for it," "It's against God's commands," "It hurts others." A Muslim or Jew, who does not recognize Jesus Christ as their Savior, could give the same response without compromising any principle of their faith.

In supplying a motive for our actions Christians are not making use of that which is distinctive to our faith. Most of the time Christians interpret the world and motivate their life using the same basic principle as the rest of the world: LAW! This is a negative way of looking at life. One might even call it "depressing."

The Biblical motive for life is God's grace and his promises. The motive for our life is supposed to be the "Good News" or "Gospel." Without this gospel revealed to us in Scripture, our natural answers to all the moral and ethical questions of life are rooted in the negative, rather than the positive. According to the apostle Paul (Rm 14:23), anything we do without reference to our faith (in the gospel), is sin!

The Christian, motivated by the gospel, ought to answer the question *"Why should Christians not steal?"* with an automatic response such as: *"I do not have to steal because God has promised to supply my needs."* This response is clearly rooted in Scripture and the gracious promises God makes to us through Christ. Rather than seeking motive in a negative, the Christian finds motive in the positive "Good News."

Cognitive therapy (CBT) is a useful tool in retraining the mind to think in positive terms, but what happens when logical reality offers no positive alternative? For instance, if you were Adolf Hitler at the end of World War II or Sadaam Hussein prior to his capture, thoughts such as "the whole world is out to get me" would not be classified as paranoid. Such thoughts would be a logical and rational interpretation of life. If you were a secular cognitive therapist and had opportunity to confront these individuals at these desperate times in life, how would you put a positive spin on their worldly outlook and relieve their depression?

Not all depressed thinking is irrational. The playwright David Ives once wrote in the New York Times, *"Considering the state of the world, why does science still consider depression an aberration? . . . Optimism is, in fact, a form of desperation that science would do well to investigate . . . Depression, let it be said, is nothing more than realism."* [59] In *"Mourning and Melancholia,"* a work dealing with the treatment of depression, Sigmund Freud states that if a patient:

> *"represents his ego to us as worthless, incapable of any achievement and morally despicable . . . He must surely be right in some way . . . It may be so far as we know, that he has come pretty near to understanding himself; we only wonder why a man has to be ill before he can be accessible to truth of this kind."* [60]

If people don't wave at you when you wave at them, maybe it is not because they didn't see you, but because they are intentionally ignoring you. Maybe you have become so repugnant to them that they want nothing to do with you. It may be a rare circumstance, but sometimes everybody does hate you and is out to get you. Sometimes, the light at the end of the tunnel has been switched off. Sometimes it is impossible to put a positive spin on things. At least, the negative seems far more reasonable and probable than the positive.

To deal with these types of issues, cognitive therapists such as David Burns must introduce a large dose of relativism into the thinking process. For instance, in dealing with anger management he writes, *"fairness is simply a perceptual interpretation, an abstraction, a self created concept . . . Who's 'right'? There is no ultimate 'true' answer . . . 'absolute fairness' does not exist."* [61] His main tool in combating perfectionism is simply an acceptance of a certain level of imperfection. The question, however, is where do we draw that line?

Biblical Christianity and many other faith systems deal with life from the perspective of absolutes, not relativism. Life itself seems to suggest that certain ideas are not negotiable. For instance, though there is no logical or scientific basis for heaven, most of the world continues to inject this idea into a system for interpreting life. The Bible tells us it is not accidental nor coincidental that so many people believe in life

---

[59]Ives, David. "In Praise of Depression" (New York Times, New York, N.Y.: Jun 17, 1981. pg. A31)

[60]Freud, Sigmund, "Collected Papers", 1917 (Translated by Joan Riviere, Vol. IV, chapter 8, "Mourning and Melancholia", pp. 155-156. London: Hogarth Press Ltd., 1952)

[61]Burns, David p. 161

after death. The Bible tells us that God (Ec 3:11) *"has also set eternity in the hearts of men."*

Morality is not one person's perspective on life. The Bible tells us that people who do not have God's written law (Rm 2:14-15) *"show that the requirements of the law are written on their hearts, their consciences also bearing witness, and their thoughts now accusing, now even defending them."*

While the techniques of cognitive therapy are useful, sometimes its principles defy an honest assessment of our life on this earth. Sometimes an honest assessment of life leads to one absolute and undeniable conclusion. Life really stinks, you are a horrible person, and there is no earthly evidence to suggest that this will ever change.

It is in these moments when it becomes clear that a faith-based approach to depression is critical. The thief on the cross, who died next to Jesus, provides an excellent example of the role that faith can play in desperate circumstances.

Study and Discuss

Read Luke 23:39-43

What is this criminal's immediate future on earth?

What is this criminal's eternal future if it is true that *"good people go to heaven and bad people go to hell?"*

How is this criminal's eternal future changed by the gospel of forgiveness purchased through Christ?

The gospel of Jesus Christ is not a logical or reasonable viewpoint that would naturally occur to this thief on the cross. In fact, based upon his current circumstances, the idea that he would dwell in eternal glory might be labeled as "delusional thinking," especially since his hope is based on the promise of someone who was falsely accused, deserted by all his friends, mocked by everyone, and dying right next to him.

The gospel or "Good News" is not only foreign to people in depressed circumstances, the gospel is foreign to the human nature we are born with. As demonstrated in our earlier exercise on the question of stealing, even Christians rarely use the gospel in responding to life.

Secular cognitive therapy is providing help to people living with depression because it helps them envision an alternate reality to the world as they have been perceiving it. However, this therapy is limited by our earthly and sinful perspective. Secular cognitive therapy cannot comfort the dying, or deal with justified guilt over the mistakes we have made in the past. This therapy can only point out realities that can be seen and touched, or encourage us to ignore certain fundamental and absolute truths of life.

While CBT should not be regarded by the Christian as the final answer to depression, its techniques, overlaid with Scriptural truth, can be used by Christians to reshape their thinking processes in conformity with the gospel of Jesus Christ. In one sense, the goal of CBT and Christianity are the same: To change the belief system by which we interpret the world around us.

How Do We Identify Our Cognitive Distortions?

There are many people who respond to the gospel centered propositions presented earlier in a negative fashion. People often ask, *"If our life is to be ruled only by promises and by grace, what is the point of God giving us laws?"* Scripture answers this question for us.

Study And Discuss

Read Romans 3:19-24; 5:20-21; 7:7-13

Can we become righteous by obeying the law?

Then why did God give us the law?

God designed us to naturally live in accordance with his will. Adam and Eve only needed one law to govern their lives until they stopped trusting God and his grace. When we live our lives completely trusting in God's grace and promises, we will not sin. The problem is, we no longer live our lives completely trusting in God's grace and promises. Such a life is completely foreign to us.

Think of God's law not as a motivational tool, but as a diagnostic tool. Through the law, God diagnoses all of our spiritual ailments. The law, however, is not the cure for these ailments. The law's function, according to Scripture, is purely diagnostic.

Study and Discuss

You go to a doctor because you are feeling sick. The doctor takes your temperature, blood pressure, and some blood tests. He comes back and says "You are sick!" Then he hands you a bill and leaves.

1) **Was the doctor acting appropriately when he administered the tests he gave to you?**

2) **In what ways has this doctor failed to do his job?**

The doctor in this example failed in at least two ways. You are sick, but you don't know what particular illness you have. Knowing this is important because it will affect your treatment. The doctor also failed in that he didn't tell you how you could be cured. The tests are valuable, but only in so far as they direct us to understand our illness and direct us to the proper cure. Apart from this use, the tests are worthless.

According to Scripture, when the law fails to drive us to the gospel, its work is worthless. God's law is a fantastic diagnostic tool, but it is powerless to cure what ails our spirit. It points out, in specific ways, our spiritual illnesses. However, unless the law causes us to seek out some aspect of God's grace, its work is useless.

God's law is not an obligation for the Christian, but a description of how people live in the light of God's grace. When we break the law, God would have a little trigger go off in our minds that says, "There is something about God's grace that I must be forgetting."

As we come into this world, this trigger mechanism in our brains is dead. We no longer understand the connection between God's law and God's grace. Instead, we naturally interpret God's law as, at best, an obligation we must perform for him, and at worst, a terrible threat. During his ministry Jesus was constantly trying to correct this misunderstanding.

Study and Discuss

Read Mark 2:23-28

How did the Pharisees understand the Sabbath?

How did Jesus understand the Sabbath?

The Pharisees understood the Sabbath law as an obligation. Jesus understood this law as a gift. The law was the same, but seen from a different viewpoint. The Pharisees misunderstanding of the law led them to accuse Jesus of breaking the Sabbath law, even when his activity was not specifically forbidden in Scripture.

There is no law in Scripture against doing miracles on the Sabbath, but each time Jesus would heal on the Sabbath the Pharisees would become agitated and accuse him of breaking the law. There is no law against raising people from the dead, but when Jesus raised Lazarus from the dead the Pharisees began their plot to kill Jesus (Jn 11:53). Because of their flawed spiritual understanding, the Pharisees perpetually put a negative spin on everything good that Jesus would do.

Christians must understand that the proper function of God's law is to help us recognize when we are drifting from grace. God gave us the law to diagnose us, but not to cure us. You will be encouraged to become familiar with the common cognitive distortions identified in CBT for the same reason. They are great diagnostic tools in the quest to bring healing to people suffering from depression and anxiety, but learning to recognize these distortions is not the cure.

While it is important to identify times when our thinking patterns are drifting from the positive to the negative, learning new ways of interpreting life is the ultimate key to defeating depression and anxiety. As we become familiar with these distorted thinking styles, we will also learn the Scriptural antidotes to apply when we catch our thoughts drifting into the negative.

It is important to remember that retraining our minds requires effort and study. Long established thought patterns cannot be broken by simply reading a book, or wishing them away. Like training the mind for any skill, practice and repetition are the keys to success. The Apostle Paul writes to the Corinthians:

> (1Co 9:24-27) *"Do you not know that in a race all the runners run, but only one gets the prize? Run in such a way as to get the prize. Everyone who competes in the games goes into strict training. They do it to get a crown that will not last; but we do it to get a crown that will last forever. Therefore I do not run like a man running aimlessly; I do not fight like a man beating the air. No, I beat my body and make it my slave so that after I have preached to others, I myself will not be disqualified for the prize."*

With this in mind we now turn our attention to investigating the common cognitive distortions and how they affect our daily lives. As noted in lesson 4, the following categories are adapted from the book by David D. Burns, *"Feeling Good: The New Mood Therapy"*, Avon Books (1999). Some of the illustrations have been slightly modified or replaced.

How Do Cognitive Distortions Affect Daily Life?

1. **ALL-OR-NOTHING THINKING:** You see things in black-and-white categories. If your performance falls short of perfect, you see yourself as a total failure.

Examples

a. You get a "B" on a test, but you usually get an "A" on everything. You label yourself a failure and drop the class.

b. *You are throwing a party. Everyone seems to enjoy themselves and leave in a good mood, but the dessert wasn't served on time. You made a mess of everything and will never throw a party again because it is just too stressful.*

c. *You ask a child to clean a room. The room looks spotless but for one item that is out of place. You stress out and yell at the child for being a slob and a lazy good for nothing.*

2. **OVER-GENERALIZATION:** You see a single negative event as a never-ending pattern of defeat.

Examples

a. *You go in for a job interview but you are not hired. You conclude that you will never be able to get a job and quit looking for work.*

b. *Your spouse is usually very punctual, but about once a month your spouse is ten or fifteen minutes late for dinner. When your spouse enters the house you exclaim "You are always late! You're never on time!"*

c. *You ask a member of the opposite sex for a date but are turned down. You say to yourself, "I'm never going to get a date, I'll be single for the rest of my life!"*

3. **MENTAL FILTER:** You pick one negative detail and dwell on it exclusively so that your vision of all reality becomes darkened, like the drop of ink that discolors the entire beaker of water.

Examples

a. *When you talk about your childhood the only events you recall are negative ones. Yet, your other family members remember you as being quite happy as a child.*

b. *You are driving home from work in heavy traffic. Several drivers wave you in as you periodically change lanes on your way home, but one driver needlessly speeds up and cuts you off. When you get home you exclaim to your family that "there are no kind drivers left in the world. Everyone is just out for themselves."*

c. *You have a good job that has provided well for your family's needs. You have been working with the same company for 18 years. Recently you were hoping for a promotion, but someone else got the job. You say to yourself, "I've just totally wasted 18 years of my life."*

4. **DISQUALIFYING THE POSITIVE:** You reject positive experiences by insisting they "don't count" for some reason or other. In this way you can maintain a negative belief that is contradicted by your everyday experiences.

Examples

a. *You studied hard for a test and got the highest grade in the class. Your instructor pulls you aside and says, "I can see from your test that you have a real grasp of this material." You respond by saying, "No, I'm just a good guesser."*

b. *You just had a professional portrait taken. Someone tells you that you look beautiful and you respond by saying, "No, the photographer is just really good at touching up stuff!" or someone tells you that you look great in a certain dress and you respond, "Yeah, it hides the fat well."*

c. *Someone evaluates a project you have been working on very positively. When a friend asks you how your evaluation went you tell them the evaluator's response but then qualify it by saying, "I think they were just trying to be nice to me."*

5. **JUMPING TO CONCLUSIONS:** You make a negative interpretation even though there are no definite facts that convincingly support your conclusion. This jumping to conclusions has two different forms.

Examples

A. **MIND READING:** You arbitrarily conclude that someone is reacting negatively to you, and you don't bother to check this out.

a. *You walk in a room and see a group of people whispering. You are convinced that they are talking negatively about you.*

b. *You have a conflict with your family or a group of close friends. You cut off the conversation that would lead to a resolution by exclaiming, "You all hate me!" and leave the room.*

c. *You are at a restaurant waiting for a date to show up who is 10 minutes late. This person seemed very excited about going out with you. You assume you did something wrong and have been stood up. You leave the restaurant as your date sits frustrated in a traffic jam.*

B. **NEGATIVE PREDICTION**: You can anticipate that things will turn out badly, and you feel convinced that your prediction is an already-established fact.

Examples

a. *You are having pain but won't go and see the doctor because you know that he is going to tell you that you have a cancer tumor and you will die soon. Why bother the doctor?*

b. *You know that you are going to fail a test so you won't waste your time studying.*

c. *You had a misunderstanding with a friend, but you refuse to talk to them and try to correct the misinformation because you know that they won't change their mind.*

6. **MAGNIFICATION OR MINIMIZATION:** You exaggerate the importance of things (such as your goof-up or someone else's achievement), or you inappropriately shrink things until they appear tiny (your good qualities or the imperfections of others).

Examples

a. *You get a pimple on your face just before a party and refuse to go because you know that everyone will be staring at you all night (magnification of your goof up).*

b. *You won't apply for a promotion because you know the other applicants. You know that you could never be as good as they are (magnification of the achievement of others and minimizing your qualities).*

c. *Your spouse just gave you a black eye in a fit of rage and you rationalize it by pointing to some failure on your part. Your child just called you every name in the book because you asked them to be home at a reasonable hour. You rationalize it by saying your child has always been over sensitive (minimizing the other person's imperfections).*

7. **EMOTIONAL REASONING:** You assume that your negative emotions necessarily reflect the way things really are: "I feel it, therefore it must be true."

Examples

a. *An alcoholic family member who drifts from job to job just coerced you into lending them $500.00 that you really couldn't afford to lend. Other family members said you shouldn't do it, and you even had thoughts that this really wasn't going to help your alcoholic family member, but you were made to feel so guilty that you did it anyway.*

b. *You are always angry because everybody around you is always trying to mess up your life.*

c. *Everyone at work tells you that you are working too hard. Yet, you refuse to take vacation time and go into work even when you are seriously ill because you are worried that someone might do your job better and you will be replaced.*

8. **SHOULD STATEMENTS:** You try to motivate yourself with "should" and "shouldn't," as if you had to be whipped and punished before you could be expected to do anything. "Musts" and "oughts" are also offenders. When you address "should" statements at yourself the emotional consequences are guilt. When you direct "should" statements toward others, you feel anger, frustration, and resentment.

Examples

a. *You are angry at work all day because your boss did not recognize the extra effort you made to finish a project! ("should" directed at others)*

b. *You feel guilty every time you look at your child because of a scar they bear from an accident. You say to yourself, "I should have never let them go out and play!" ("should" directed at self)*

c. *You were busy doing a million things other people had asked you to do. Somebody becomes angry at you for the one thing you didn't get done after an exhausting day. You feel both guilty and frustrated. You say to yourself, "I know I should have done that first!" ("should" directed at self and others)*

9. **LABELING AND MISLABELING:** This is an extreme form of over-generalization. Instead of describing your error, you attach a negative label to yourself. "I'm a loser." When someone else's behavior rubs you the wrong way, you attach a negative label to him: "He's a louse!" Mislabeling involves describing an event with language that is highly colored and emotionally loaded.

    a. *Your spouse comes home and asks if dinner will be ready soon. You haven't started anything because you were busy with other family obligations (transporting children, helping with projects, cleaning). You mumble aloud, "No, its not. I'm just a lousy . . . (wife/husband)!"*

    b. *Your child has not cleaned their room in the last week. You enter the bedroom, look around, and say, "You are such a slob!"*

    c. *Someone tries to explain some (homework, work skill, etc.) to you and you do not understand the concept well after the first explanation. You exclaim, "I'm so stupid!"*

10. **PERSONALIZATION**: You see yourself as the cause of some negative external event, which in fact you were not primarily responsible for.

a. *When you were a young child, your parents got divorced and you thought you must have done something wrong that made this happen.*

b. *Your child is doing poorly in school. You blame yourself for not spending enough time with the child.*

c. *Someone dies from a heart attack. You blame yourself for their death because you did not react quickly enough, you were out shopping and should have been home, you didn't perform CPR properly, or didn't encourage that person to go to a doctor when they had mentioned they weren't feeling well.*

These are the distortions that cognitive therapists have commonly identified as the root cause for depression and anxiety. There may have been times as you read through the examples that you said to yourself, "This is not a distortion, it is the reality." You may have thought that the feelings expressed by people in these examples were justifiable based on the circumstances that were described. Some of the thought patterns may have been more typical of the way you think than others.

It is important to remember that all people have the types of thoughts described above at one time or another. The difference in depression is that people become locked into certain styles of thinking and cannot envision alternatives.

People suffering from phobias seem to have a direct mental line between the fear center of the brain and the image of a spider or mouse. Likewise, people suffering from depression lock in a certain way of processing information from the world around them. Those suffering from depression lose the ability to choose between alternate methods of interpreting a specific event or situation. All information gets shoved down the same mental pipeline regardless of circumstances and evidence to the contrary.

Changing the way our brain works is both a mental and spiritual process. It involves retraining the brain to use a more logical approach to interpret events, and the work of the Holy Spirit in our hearts to create faith in certain truths that cannot be proven. These truths may seem to be "unreasonable" to logic and contrary to all earthly evidence, yet they are life changing truths that we learn to cherish.

How are Spiritual Truths Unreasonable?

At the beginning of this lesson you were asked the simple question, "Can you *in some way* speak of yourself as being perfect (Yes or No)?" Chances are you answered "No!" Most people do. It is, after all, common knowledge in our culture that "Nobody is perfect!"

When you look at your life you don't see perfection. Rather, you see mistakes, failures, or what the Bible calls "sin!" How can anyone, based on any human logic or earthly evidence, claim perfection? Faith, however, is not based on human logic or earthly evidence. As the author of Hebrews declares (Heb 11:1) *"Now faith is being sure of what we hope for and certain of what we do not see."* By faith we hold to certain truths that cannot be proven, but can literally change our lives.

You were also asked the question at the beginning of this lesson "Have you been baptized?" Chances are that some of you answered this question positively.

Study and Discuss

Read Acts 2:37-39; 22:16 and Ephesians 5:25-27

What is the function of baptism?

If baptism does what the Bible says, what has happened to the sins of the baptized person?

Can the baptized person in some way speak of themself as being perfect?

"In some way", in the only way that really matters, the person who is connected to Christ by baptism and faith is perfect. In the cross of Christ our sins have been paid for. His blood has washed them away.

The function of faith is to lay hold of this message and apply it to our lives. The function of baptism is to make this good news more certain through an objective event. How can I be certain that Christ's death was meant for me? In baptism, God takes an event that took place roughly 2000 years ago and applies it to me personally in the here and now! God so loved the world, becomes God so loved me.

No amount of human logic or reason can validate these truths. No modern earthly evidence can be brought forth in support of these facts. This truth is not made part of our life through mental efforts. Rather, it is a truth taught by the Spirit as he works in our hearts through God's word and the sacraments.

The knowledge that we have been made perfect in Christ is life changing. Such knowledge forever changes how we deal with issues of sin and guilt, but only when we trust in it, and then apply this knowledge to our daily lives. For far too many Christians, this knowledge is applicable only to the process of dying, and has nothing to do with how we live.

Have you ever lied to try to cover up a sin? Have you ever been reluctant to do something because you were afraid you might make a mistake? Did someone ever make you do something you felt was wrong because they laid a big guilt trip on you?

Perfect people would never do the things described above. Perfect people have nothing to cover up. Perfect people don't fear making mistakes. Perfect people are never motivated by guilt. Yet, such actions are committed every day by Christians around the world who say that they believe in Jesus and that their sins have been washed away.

While you may know that Jesus died on the cross to save you from your sins, and while this knowledge will bring you eternal salvation, you may not be experiencing the full benefits of this knowledge here and now because you have not learned how to use it as a governing principle for daily life. The lessons which follow are intended to help you grow in this ability, that you might experience more of the fruits of the spirit such as joy and peace in your life.

Lesson 5 ~ Weekly Activities

Review Exercise

In addition to the normal focus on your devotional life, exercise, diet, and sleep patterns, you are encouraged to complete this review exercise. Try to find a time this week to share the list of cognitive distortions with someone you know (perhaps your support partner, some family members, or your pastor). It is very important that others be involved in this activity. The goal of this activity is to help you develop new ways of interpreting situations and events. In this process, having another point of view is extremely helpful.

As you begin this activity, you should also have available a set of cards that came with your book entitled:

Law~Gospel Thinking Cards

These cards list the 10 cognitive distortions and the law and gospel foundations behind these thinking styles. Review these cards and refer to them whenever you try to identify your cognitive distortions and the positive thinking alternatives.

When you begin this activity, read aloud the following instructions:

1. *Inform everyone present at the meeting that you will be reading a list of "cognitive distortions" that are common to all people. Explain to everyone that you need to study this list to help yourself overcome depression.*

    a. *Inform everyone that, after reading the list, you will give an example of how you have used one of these distortions.*

    b. *Ask everyone if they would help you by giving one example in their life where they may have used one of these distortions. No one is obligated to do this if it makes them feel uncomfortable.*

    c. *Inform everyone that it is important that no one give an example of how someone else may have used one of these distortions.*

    d. *Inform everyone that after you have come up with several examples of distorted thinking, you will analyze these thoughts together and try to identify alternative ways of interpreting the events or situations that prompted these thoughts.*

2. *Review the list with everyone present. After reading the examples under each category ask everyone if they understood the examples.*
3. *Give a personal example of when you may have used one of these distortions.*
4. *Ask others if they would be willing to give an example from their own life describing when they used one of these distortions.*
5. *With the group, pick at least two distortions to be analyzed. For this purpose refer to page A15 in the Appendix entitled:*

ANALYZING COGNITIVE DISTORTIONS ~ WEEK 5

6. *On this page write down two events or situations that prompted distorted thinking. Follow the instructions for analyzing your thoughts. Remember that the gospel is always centered in God's love, grace, and promises. The gospel IS NOT what God tells YOU to do. The gospel IS what God says HE will do. Refer to the LAW~GOSPEL THINKING CARDS for help in identifying the gospel.*

Remember that all people use these distortions at one time or another, but in depression these distortions become far more common place. This is why it is important to practice identifying these distortions in your life and also to practice the identification of positive, gospel centered, alternatives to the distorted thinking. If you have difficulty in understanding this activity refer to the sample (**Appendix** p. A14)

CARING FOR THE BODY AND SPIRIT GOD GAVE ME

Do not neglect your body as we focus on mind and spirit issues. Continue to track and discuss with others the additional activities you are doing. This includes your sleep patterns, diet, exercise, as well as altering other daily activities (spending more time talking, playing music, reading, or adding other activities to your day).

For your devotional time this week you are encouraged to read at least one chapter a day from Paul's Epistle to the Galatians. In addition, read through the following scriptural selections and answer the questions associated with those readings. It is recommended that you spread these readings throughout the week, rather than doing them all at once, to keep your mind and spirit focused on the gospel.

Scripture Reading

Day 2 ~ Read Hebrews 11:1 - 12:3

What definition of faith is given in verse 1?

What foolish act (by the world's standards) did Noah undertake because he trusted in God?

List at least two acts that Abraham undertook, based upon his trust in God, that would seem foolish in the eyes of most people?

Day 4 ~ Read Numbers 13:17 - 14:24

What kind of land was God offering to the people of Israel? (see 13:27)

How did Joshua and Caleb's action plan differ from the rest of the people who had gone to spy out the land and why? (see 13:30, 14:6-9)

Whose advice did the people of Israel eventually follow and why do you think they followed that advice?

Day 6 ~ Read 1 Corinthians 10:13

Has anything ever happened to you that has not happened to others?

What promise does God make as you face trials and troubles in life?

How can faith in this promise change the way we face our problems?

- NOTES -

- NOTES -

Lesson 6
The Distortions of "All or Nothing" and "Over-Generalization"

What's the Point? *All future lessons zero in on specific cognitive distortions and the positive, gospel centered, solutions to these styles of thinking. This lesson focuses on "All or Nothing" thinking and "Over-Generalization," identifying the negative impact these distortions have and the positive gospel principles that help us overcome these thinking styles.*

How Can I Become Perfect?

In our last lesson we identified several patterns of thinking that are characteristic of people suffering from depression. In this and future lessons we deal more specifically with each cognitive distortion and try to identify specific gospel promises that will help us change our mental outlook from the negative to the positive.

In carrying out this process it is important for us to fully comprehend the logic behind these distorted thinking styles. To combat the enemies of our mind, we must first, according to the old adage, "know thine enemy!" To review the first cognitive distortion:

1. ALL-OR-NOTHING THINKING

You see things in black-and-white categories. If your performance falls short of perfect, you see yourself as a total failure.

Examples

a. *You get a "B" on a test, but you usually get an "A" on everything. You label yourself a failure and drop the class.*

b. *You are throwing a party. Everyone seems to enjoy themselves and leave in a good mood, but the dessert wasn't served on time. You made a mess of everything and will never throw a party again because it is just too stressful.*

c. *You ask a child to clean a room. The room looks spotless but for one item that is out of place. You stress out and yell at the child for being a slob and a lazy good for nothing.*

All or nothing thinking is a form of perfectionism. The pursuit of perfection can take two different paths. Along one path, individuals define their own standards of perfection. These people become the over achievers, the people who must control everything in their environment, the neat freaks, and so on. When the world around these individuals does not conform to their standards of perfection, they will do everything in their power to make the world conform.

Failing to achieve conformity will result in great frustration and/or anger. People like this will generally make it obvious to others when they are failing in their pursuit of perfection with emotional outbursts. Those who are caught up in this form of thinking endlessly snatch defeat from the jaws of victory. Nothing is ever good enough. Things could always be better, because in this sinful world, nothing is perfect.

Another, perhaps less obvious pursuit of perfectionism, is practiced by those individuals who allow others to set the standards for achievement in their life. These are the people pleasers, the overly compliant, and frequently the victims of abuse. Their goal is to be thought of perfectly by others, and they will often go to great lengths to appease the whims of others. When they cannot please someone else, they also become frustrated and angry, but these emotions are internalized and buried. To reveal these emotions would be counter productive (in their minds) to their goal of pleasing others.

The origins of this style of thinking might be found in parents who placed high expectations along with ample doses of criticism upon their children. For instance, their child gets an "A" on a school project and brings it home beaming with pride, but the parent can't stop with praise for the achievement, but moves on to pointing out several alternatives for improvement.

In adolescence, a time period when extreme life changes are taking place, such thinking could be influenced by peer groups where the teen is surrounded by people who always seem to achieve slightly more. Perhaps the teen has an over achieving sibling, a "golden child," that they always feel they are being compared to. Whatever family or social factors lie behind this type of thinking, there is also a spiritual side to this thinking.

Study and Discuss

Read Matthew 5:44-48

What standard of achievement does God have for us?

Read Galatians 5:19-21

What is the penalty for failing to live according to God's standards?

Biblically speaking "all or nothing" is not a distorted form of thinking. "All or nothing" is the reality of our relationship with God apart from the gospel of Jesus Christ. This form of thinking naturally arises if we are honest with ourselves about our sin. The problem with "all or nothing" thinking is not the desire to seek perfection, but the method by which we pursue it.

Study and Discuss

Read Romans 3:10-20 and Isaiah 64:6

Can anyone achieve perfection on their own?

Do any of our deeds measure up to God's standards of righteousness?

The righteous standards of God's law are "all or nothing." When we try to find satisfaction in life through our own efforts, we always fall short. We cannot establish our righteousness by our own efforts because we are not perfect, and God requires perfection. In his mercy, however, God has provided another way to achieve righteousness.

Most therapists are ill-equipped to point out God's path to total righteousness, and if publicly funded, therapists are even forbidden by law to discuss this method. God has given us the righteousness of Christ as a substitute for our own.

In our last lesson we read about the thief who died on a cross next to Jesus (Lk 23:39-43). This thief hoped for eternal glory in paradise, but not based upon who he was or anything he had done. This *"thief on the cross"* rested his hope of glory in a promise made to him by Jesus. A promise rooted in God's grace, not our efforts.

Without the gospel "proving our worth," building our "self-esteem," proving that we "are someone special," can only be accomplished through our own efforts or deeds. The problem is that at our best, we're never that good.

The law of God tells us that no matter how hard we try, we will always fall short of his glory and his demands. No matter how hard you try, you are never going to be good enough, smart enough, nice enough, or whatever else you are trying to be. Under the law, we will always stand condemned as sinners.

Gospel oriented thinking gives up on the doomed effort to "prove our worth" to ourselves, parents, spouse, and God. Gospel oriented thinking rests our sense of worth and accomplishment in the righteousness that Christ has given as a free gift to all who believe. You are perfect, just the way you are, not by your own effort, but through the work of Christ on the cross.

Relieved from the all consuming pressure of the law and its demands, life for the Christian, living under the Spirit, changes. The Scriptural descriptions of life under the Spirit are not goals we must achieve! Rather, they are the "fruits" that we will experience in increasing measure as we as live our lives under the Gospel.

Study and Discuss

Read Romans 3:21-28

How does a person become righteous?

Read Galatians 5:22-25

How is life under the Spirit different from life under the law?

The Christian approach to "all or nothing" thinking differs from secular cognitive therapy in that it validates the reality that life ultimately is all or nothing. God's demand for righteousness is not defined in a color scheme dominated by shades of gray. Christianity is rooted in black and white. It is not enough that we tried hard or did our best. God demands perfection! Jesus' encounter with the rich young man provides a classic example of this principle.

Study and Discuss

Read Luke 18:18-27

What question does this rich ruler ask of Jesus?

Did this rich ruler think that he was living a good life?

What caused the rich ruler to become depressed?

What is impossible for us?

What is possible for God?

The illustration above demonstrates the proper use of the law. The law, with its unyielding demands, is designed to make us despair of the doomed attempt to establish our righteousness through our own efforts. The proper function of the law is to drive us to the gospel and into the arms of a loving and forgiving heavenly Father. In the gospel, righteousness is based on pure grace and received by simple faith in Christ. God delivers us from a hopeless condition of imperfection through the forgiveness we have in Christ.

Christians, relying on the gospel, have nothing to prove to anyone. We can speak of ourselves as being perfect, not by our own actions, but by the saving action of God in Jesus Christ. In baptism, our sins are washed away by the blood of Jesus.

The Christian will still do righteous acts, but from a fundamentally different motivation. Since gospel motivated Christians have nothing to prove, it is not a big deal if they somehow fall short of someone's expectations during the course of the day, including their own.

There is no failure, no sin, no imperfection that can change God's love for us in Christ Jesus. The Christian strives for righteousness in his or her life because that is the natural pursuit of the heart set free from fear, worry, guilt and doubt through faith in the gospel. The Christian doesn't steal, not because the Bible says "Thou shalt not!", but because the Christian knows that God will provide.

The gospel helps Christians rightly prioritize their actions and goals. Without the gospel sinful man is always seeking that elusive trophy by which we can claim "I'm somebody!" When we don't find enough support for this concept in relationships, particularly with parents and spouses, our sinful ego tries to invent other methods by which we can prop ourselves up.

We were designed by God to find fulfillment in the pursuit of love, but work, hobbies, cleanliness, academics, sports, or other pursuits often become so large in our lives that our relationships with others take second or even last place. Somewhat meaningless activities become the avenues where people pursue their perfection because they cannot achieve perfection in their marriage, family life, or social interaction with their peers.

The extraordinary effort required for achievement in these artificial measures of our worth, become a barrier to fulfilling our true purpose in life; that is, to love one another. Relationships with family and friends are set aside to make room for our other pursuits. These vain pursuits then are used by Satan to set us up for unbearable despair.

Consider for instance the baseball player, or Olympic athlete, whose entire life is devoted to making it to the pro's, or winning the gold medal. What happens when through accident or injury that person can no longer pursue this goal. When something we "do" becomes the focal point of our self-worth, failure in this arena evokes feelings of utter despair and hopelessness. This overwhelming despair also afflicts those who have sought perfection in trying to please others.

What happens to the person who has spent a life time trying to please others at their own expense, but despite all their efforts, that person's marriage ends in failure? What happens when someone spends a lifetime focused on family, but the family disintegrates? Again, utter despair results. Such individuals often see their life as a total failure.

Those who experience life-altering events often sink into deep depression. Life becomes meaningless. If there was some individual or institution that stood in the way of success, rage and anger can erupt. Devastating events such as suicide or homicidal rampages are often the outcome when life is radically changed for the worse.

The gospel of Jesus Christ changes us because it frees us from the pursuit of perfection. Without the unrelenting drive to "prove" who we are or to "measure up" to the expectations of others, the Christian naturally knows what matters, and what doesn't.

When we are condemned by God's word, family, or friends for having our priorities messed up, we need to realize that the solution is not found in doing something different, but believing something different. We need to change mental gears and slip out of the "law" mode of trying to achieve some standard or level to satisfy others, and slip into the "gospel" mode which recognizes that all requirements placed upon us have been satisfied in Christ. There is nothing to prove to anyone.

As we deal with "all or nothing" thinking, the Christian focuses on confession and the gift of perfection God has given us through Christ.

Christians should not be satisfied with shades of gray, but should recognize the glorious white robes we have been clothed with. Robes made white in the blood of the lamb.

Study and Discuss

Read Psalm 18:32; 51:7; Colossians 1:28; Revelation 7:13-14 and Hebrews 10:11-14

What is our condition in Christ Jesus?

Can you, in some way, say that you are perfect?

How Does God Overcome So Much Evil?

There is much that is evil in this world. Sometimes people can become so overwhelmed by what is wrong with the world that they become blind to the goodness of God that surrounds us. We call this type of thinking "Over-Generalization." To review:

2. OVER-GENERALIZATION

You see a single negative event as a never-ending pattern of defeat.

Examples

a. *You go in for a job interview but you are not hired. You conclude that you will never be able to get a job and quit looking for work.*

b. *Your spouse is usually very punctual, but about once a month your spouse is ten or fifteen minutes late for dinner. When your spouse enters the house you exclaim, "You are always late! You're never on time!"*

c. *You ask a member of the opposite sex for a date but are turned down. You say to yourself, "I'm never going to get a date, I'll be single for the rest of my life!"*

In this form of thinking, individuals tend to make sweeping generalizations from a single negative experience. Each failure, each struggle, is interpreted to mean that all future events and all future efforts will yield the same negative result.

Over-generalization can extend to our understanding of relationships. If we have a negative experience with one person in a group, we may generalize that all people in the group have the same attitude. If one person becomes angry with me, "Everybody hates me!"

This attitude quickly evolves into a "Why should I even try?" mentality and an ever shrinking sphere of life experiences. Individuals who over-generalize exhaust their family and friends because of the continued effort that must be exerted in encouraging even simple tasks of life. The frustration of family, friends and co-workers, adds to the individual's own negative opinion of themselves.

Such thinking can evolve out of a succession of negative experiences in life. The idea that "everything seems to be going wrong" may be an accurate interpretation of a particular period in life. For instance, if Sadaam Hussein thought everybody was out to get him when the U.S. invaded Iraq and that there was no one he could trust, he was not over-generalizing.

People with abnormal physical or mental characteristics may not be over-generalizing when they feel everyone is looking at them. Conversations with new acquaintances may inevitably turn to, "So how did that happen to you?"

In certain dysfunctional family settings, individual children are sometimes singled out as the "bad one." Whenever a conflict occurs, or a problem arises, the blame always falls on one child regardless of evidence to the contrary. Every correction leads to some comparison, "Why can't you be more like . . . ?"

Within all kinds of social settings, pecking orders are established with certain individuals rising to the top and others falling to the bottom. If an individual's family experience and peer experience always point to failure on their part, it seems perfectly natural to over-generalize and presume that other life experiences will always end up being negative. Scripturally speaking, there is support for this type of negative thinking.

Study and Discuss

Read Psalm 14:2-3 and Romans 3:10-12

From God's point of view is there anyone who naturally seeks him?

Read Romans 7:18-19

Does the apostle Paul see himself as capable of doing anything right?

If these were the only words God had given us in Scripture, we would assume that everyone is headed straight for hell and that there is no point to life. In secular CBT people are challenged to believe that not all events will be negative. CBT challenges people to believe that while some things may be bad, not everything is bad. From a scriptural point of view, however, it is not irrational to believe that there is something negative in everything.

From the scriptural perspective of the law, expecting a negative outcome to any of our efforts is not twisted thinking, but established fact. To God, (Is 64:6) *"all our righteous acts are like filthy rags."* Scripture, however, also offers to us a different way of looking at life: a gospel perspective.

The gospel perspective is not that there are some things that are bad and some things that are good. Through the gospel God enables us to find something good in everything. Through faith in Christ the Christian doesn't see just some things as good, but learns that in everything that seems negative, God can make a positive. While frequent and wide spread failure may be our life experience, the gospel enables us to see these experiences in a new and positive light.

Study and Discuss

Read Romans 8:24-28

In what things is God at work for good?

What is the "good" for which God works? (See also Mt 6:33)

Read Matthew 5:3-12

What "negative" experiences are called blessed?

Read 1 Corinthians 1:23-31

Who does God choose as his witnesses?

The supreme example of God bringing blessing out of what seems negative is the cross of Jesus Christ. In Christ, God takes the horrific death of an innocent person, mocked by his own nation, deserted by his closest friends, and turns it into the salvation of the world. If God can bring a blessing out of this event, he can also transform those things which are negative in our life and bring about a blessing.

When we experience negative events in our life, God invites us to come to him in prayer, to search the scriptures, and to ponder how that negative event might be used for good; that is, the proclamation of God's amazing grace to us in Jesus Christ. Paul demonstrates this manner of thinking particularly in the book of Philippians which we read as part of our weekly activities in Lesson 1.

Study and Discuss

Read Philippians 1:12-14

What is the negative in Paul's life?

How has this negative become a positive?

Read Philippians 1:15-18

What is the negative in Paul's life?

How has this negative become a positive?

Read Philippians 1:20-26

What two possibilities face the apostle Paul?

Why is neither possibility seen as a negative?

Read Philippians 4:6

What does every prayer of the apostle Paul include?

Paul demonstrated an amazing ability to find positive even in that which appeared to be totally negative and hopeless. The positive, however, was always connected to God's gracious purpose for Paul's life. That purpose was to both eternally save Paul, and to use Paul to bring others to saving faith in Christ.

Where the average person would see only doom and gloom, Paul saw positives when looking through the eyes of Christ and the mission that God has given to every Christian. One of the best Scriptural examples of how life as seen through Christ differs from life as seen through our sinful nature, is found in the encounter between Jesus and a man who was born blind.

Study and Discuss

Read John 9:1-12, 35-39

What were the only two explanations for this man's blindness offered by the disciples?

What explanation for this blindness did Jesus offer?

Besides being cured of blindness, what positive results grew out of this man being born blind?

It's easy to over-generalize from the negative, because in a sinful world the negative surrounds us. God however, in his grace, is able to take even that which is negative and transform it. (Rm 8:28) *"And we know that in all things God works for the good of those who love him, who have been called according to his purpose."*

As sinners we are programmed to see the negative. "Why is a man born blind?" The disciples could only see two options, either this man sinned or his parents sinned. Over-generalization comes easily. However, through faith in Christ a new reality dawns.

In everything negative, God can bring a blessing. The challenge to our mind is not to simply see some things as positive and some things as negative, but to find the positive (the "good") in all things. However, in order to find that "good," we must redefine the purpose and meaning of our lives according to God's plan.

Individuals often struggle to identify their "purpose" in this life. People often ask, "Why did God put me here?" Romans 8:28, quoted earlier, is frequently misunderstood because it is quoted by Christians without providing the proper biblical context. Note that this verse does not offer "good" to everyone for every reason.

Finding "good" in all things requires us to be in tune with God's purpose for our life. If your definition of "good" is limited to, for instance, simply getting a job, the realities of life may be that you will never experience this particular good. If Paul, in chains in prison, had defined good as simply getting out of prison, he may never have experienced that specifically defined good.

Paul found blessings in all things only because he interpreted life through Christ and the work of his kingdom. For Paul death was transformed into something which was "better by far" through Christ. Before our eyes are opened to the good which is always present, the Christian must train their mind to consider how each event might be used to bear witness to Christ, or to keep us close to Christ. Even Paul, who seems like the eternal optimist, struggled in doing this.

Study and Discuss

Read 2 Corinthians 12:6-9

Did Paul initially understand this thorn as a blessing?

What was Paul's initial prayer regarding this thorn?

How did God's revelation change Paul's attitude toward this thorn?

After God revealed his purpose, Paul stopped praying that God would remove this thorn (whatever it was). Instead, Paul began to brag about his thorn in the flesh. Through revelation, this liability was transformed into an asset. Paul is not unique in making these kinds of discoveries.

Throughout history many people with physical and mental disabilities have served as inspirations to thousands, not because they over achieved in comparison to others, but simply by the way they dealt with their infirmities. One famous individual that comes to mind is Helen Keller.

Helen Keller was a deaf and blind woman born in 1880. She became a leading advocate for civil rights, human dignity, care for the disabled, and much more. Had her speeches and writings come from a person of normal background, they may never have been published, but because of her infirmities, she became world famous.

Joe Tye is an inspirational speaker and author of the book *"Never Fear, Never Quit.*" When visiting with people who have recovered from life changing trauma he would often ask, "If given the chance to be the person you are, having experienced your trauma, or being the person you were and avoiding the trauma, which would you choose?" The overwhelming response of people to that question was to choose the trauma because of the positive way it had changed their lives.

Through Christ, every liability of ours can be turned into an asset. Even for people like the apostle Paul, this manner of thinking does not come naturally. Our sinful nature locks on to the negative, and proceeds to generalize from one negative to more negatives.

To combat this process we need to refocus our goals in life, and then ask God how each negative experience can be used to strengthen us in our faith and expand our witness to God's saving grace. Once this focus has changed, our weaknesses become strengths, and our defeats become victories.

Addressing the greatest negative of all, death, Paul writes:

> (1 Co 15:54-58) *"Death has been swallowed up in victory. Where, O death, is your victory? Where, O death, is your sting?" The sting of death is sin, and the power of sin is the law. But thanks be to God! He gives us the victory through our Lord Jesus Christ. Therefore, my dear brothers, stand firm. Let nothing move you. Always give yourselves fully to the work of the Lord, because you know that your labor in the Lord is not in vain."*

Death was God's punishment for our sin and rebellion. Yet, through the death of Christ, God turned this negative into a positive. If Christ can turn death into a positive, there is nothing that lies beyond the reach of God that cannot be turned into a positive. The solution to "over-generalization" is not to see some things as negative and some things as positive. The solution to "over-generalization" is the belief that God can transform any negative into a positive when we use it to serve the advancement of the gospel and the kingdom of Christ.

Lesson 6 ~ Weekly Activities

This and subsequent lessons follow a consistent pattern of weekly activities. One of these activities is essential to changing your thinking patterns. It involves use of the exercises from the **Appendix** entitled:

Analyzing Cognitive Distortions

Owners of this book and resident members of their household may freely copy these pages from the appendix for their personal use. If you find the writing space inadequate, you may need to construct your own pages for this activity or enlarge them on a copier.

On a daily basis, you will identify at least one cognitive distortion. Follow the process we practiced in Lesson 5 in analyzing the distortion. Always seek out an aspect of God's love and promises to help you overcome each distortion.

Constant attention to your thinking styles will help you better recognize distorted, negative thinking, and replace it with gospel centered positive thinking. Retraining your brain takes practice! Use the Law ~ Gospel Thinking Cards to help you identify these distortions and to try and identify gospel centered alternatives. Keep these cards handy during the day when you catch yourself slipping into destructive thought patterns.

Caring for the Body and Spirit God Gave me

The second part of your weekly activities will be to continue to monitor and improve upon your diet, exercise, sleep, and devotion regimen. Remember that you are body, mind, and spirit. Do not neglect your body as we focus on mind and spirit issues. Include the following devotional exercises for your spirit.

Scripture Reading

Read some of Paul's letter to the Romans during this week (2-3 chapters a day). In addition, do the following readings on their recommended days and answer the questions associated with them.

Day 2 ~ Read Colossians 3:12 - 4:2

What is one of the keys to the life of Christian peace that Paul gives in 3:15, 17 & 4:2?

Is thankfulness a command you must follow to make God happy, or is it the ability to recognize everything that God is doing for you?

Read Ecclesiastes 7:14-21

Can anyone achieve perfection in everything?

According to these words of Scripture, is the pursuit of perfection always good for us?

Day 4 ~ Read John 15:3; Hebrews 10:10; Romans 5:19

How and when do we become righteous?

How might such knowledge affect us when we are invited to give our advice in a situation where the "right" or "wrong" decision is not clear?

If you believed that righteousness was something you achieved on your own, would you be as likely to give advice in a situation where the "right" or "wrong" decision was not clear?

Day 6

Martin Luther (the 15th century reformer) had a wonderful saying brought about through his knowledge of the gospel. The Latin version is "pecca fortiter." Roughly translated it meant, "Sin boldly." Luther did not mean that we should actively choose sin. However, our life presents us with many situations where the "right" or "wrong" choice is not immediately evident. Sometimes we do not have all the facts needed to make the "right" decision, but a decision needs to be made NOW!

In such situations Luther offered the advice that we should prayerfully make up our minds trying our best to do God's will and to move forward with all boldness, fearing nothing. If, however, we find out later that we have done wrong, we should immediately confess our sin, receive forgiveness, and move on.

In Luther's day it was the fear of sinning that had driven many people into monasteries. It was believed that a more holy life could be achieved by being totally separated from worldly influences. In some of these monasteries the monks would even take vows of silence, to avoid saying anything wrong. Women were never allowed inside, to avoid the temptation of lust.

This attempt to achieve righteousness through separation was not unique to Luther's era. In Jesus' day there was a group of separatists called the "Essenes." They believed it was impossible to live a righteous life in the world of their day, so they separated themselves into religious communes in the desert areas near the Jordan river. They are known to us today through the "Dead Sea Scrolls" which they hid in caves near their communes. More familiar to us from Scripture are the Pharisees, who in the pursuit of righteousness would not enter into a Gentile's house for fear they might touch something "unclean."

Read Matthew 9:11-13

How did the fear of doing the wrong thing affect the Pharisees' ability to show God's mercy to others?

Read Numbers 19:11-12 and Luke 10:30-32

How does the Old Testament regulation in Numbers 19 help explain the behavior of the Levite and the Priest?

How does the good news of forgiveness help us to avoid a "separation" mentality in the pursuit of righteousness?

- NOTES -

Lesson 7
The Distortions of "Mental Filters" and "Disqualifying the Positive"

What's the Point? *This lesson focuses on the distortions of negative "mental filters" and the tendency to "disqualify the positive." Using gospel principles we are enabled to focus on and give thanks for the blessings God daily bestows upon us.*

WHAT EVENTS IN LIFE DO WE FOCUS ON?

A negative "mental filter" differs from "over-generalization" in the way that stereotyping differs from forgetfulness. "Over-generalization" allows one negative event to negatively color future expectations or unknown factors in the world as we interpret it. *"If A is negative, then B through Z will probably be negative also!"* When using a negative mental filter the process is more *"I don't care if B through Z is positive! Since A was negative, that's all I'm going to think about!"* To review from our earlier discussion:

3. MENTAL FILTER

You pick one negative detail and dwell on it exclusively so that your vision of all reality becomes darkened, like the drop of ink that discolors the entire beaker of water.

Examples

a. *When you talk about your childhood the only events you recall are negative ones. Yet, your other family members remember you as being quite happy as a child.*

b. *You are driving home from work in heavy traffic. Several drivers wave you in as you periodically change lanes on your way home, but one driver needlessly speeds up and cuts you off. When you get home you exclaim to your family that "Every single driver on the road is an inconsiderate maniac. Everyone is out for themselves."*

c. *You have a good job that has provided well for your family's needs. You have been working with the same company for 18 years. Recently you were hoping for a promotion, but someone else got the job. You say to yourself, "I've just totally wasted 18 years of my life."*

In an earlier lesson we discussed experiments that show how our current mood affects what we recall about previous experiences and what we learn from new experiences. Memories are associated with feelings. People in a negative mood tend to recall more negative experiences from their recent past than people in a positive mood. People who memorize a random set of facts, recall those facts better when their current mood matches the mood they were in when they first memorized those facts.

When you are experiencing depression, the natural tendency of the mind is to filter out positive experiences from the past and present and focus more on negative experiences. This has the effect of making you feel even more depressed. The challenge in depression is twofold. As we discussed in the section on "over-generalization," it helps tremendously to realize that even in our negative experiences God is working for our blessing. Scripture, however, also challenges us to work on our mental focus.

Study and Discuss

Read Philippians 4:8-9

What should be the focus of our thoughts?

What is the result of this kind of focus in our life?

Read 1 Corinthians 13:4-7

What does love focus on in other people?

While God can work good things through what appears to be negative, he also surrounds us each day with obvious blessings. God wants us to focus on these positive blessings, but our sinful human nature has a propensity to focus on the negative.

The news media offers ample evidence of this tendency to focus on the negative. An individual may quietly go about doing many good deeds for years and never make the news. However, if that person commits some grievous sin, their life suddenly becomes newsworthy.

In our personal relationships "gossip" or "slander" are often common place. Gossip is conversation which focuses on the negative in others with no intention to resolve problems or help the person who is the object of conversation. Gossip is consistently condemned in Scripture because it is divisive, promotes quarrels, and destroys relationships (Lv 19:16, Pr 20:19, Tit 3:1-2, Ja 4:11).

At times it is useful to discuss negative events or our own negative qualities, but the question we must always ask is, "to what end?" When we are discussing our own faults, the faults of others, problems we experience in life, or the problems that are so prevalent in the world, the goal should be to discover God's grace in those situations, or how we can share the good news of God's grace with someone else. This fits in with God's purpose for our life on this earth. However, this is not the agenda which normally drives our focus on the negative.

During the devastation following hurricane Katrina, much of the world sat for hours on end transfixed by televison images of pain, suffering, and destruction. Being made aware of this tremendous tragedy motivated many people to wonderful acts of charity and kindness. However, the huge volume of time that people spent pondering the images from the gulf coast was not always for a saving or useful purpose.

Often, our focus on tragedy is more akin to the thrill of watching a good horror picture. We sit transfixed and in awe of the destructive power of nature. The goal of our fixation is not to build our trust in God's grace and his power to save. Instead, we build our fear of events beyond our control and our own sense of helplessness. The longer we fixate on the destruction the less we say, "God is good!" and the more we say, "How could God let such things happen?"

What is the function of your focus on negative events? Is it driving you to call into question God's grace, or helping you to see how he helps us in our time of trouble? Do you focus on negative events to discover ways to share God's grace with others, or does that focus lead you to feel paralyzed in the face of so many troubles?

The starfish story by Loren Eiseley serves as a useful illustration of how mental focus affects our behavior.[62] The story describes an encounter between an older man and young boy on the ocean shore after a storm. The young boy was tossing starfish back into the sea. As the older man scanned up and down the shore he saw thousands upon thousands of starfish. As he fixated on the countless thousands of starfish that would die, he questioned the usefulness of the boy's endeavor. The question was put forth, "What difference does it make? They're all going to die anyway." As the boy tossed another starfish into the ocean he replied, "It will make a difference to this one."

Do we focus on what can be done or on what can't be done? Do we focus on what God has given us or on the things that we don't have. One of Jesus' parables clearly demonstrates how our mental focus can change a positive event into a negative event.

Study and Discuss

Read Matthew 20:1-15

How do you think the workers hired first initially felt when they got a job?

What change in mental focus caused the workers hired first to become upset?

How did the landowner's interpretation of his actions differ from the workers' interpretation?

The grace of God always surrounds us, but our mental focus can sometimes keep us from seeing his generosity. There are also times when, as creatures, we simply are not privy to all the ways and means

---

[62]Eiseley, Loren C., "The Star Thrower" (New York: Harcourt Brace Jovanovich, 1978, pp. 171-184)

through which God may be blessing us. While God is always at work in our lives for a good purpose (Rm 8:26-28), that doesn't mean that we can always discern precisely how God will use a particular event for our blessing.

Most people can look back upon some event in their life which, at the time, seemed to be purely negative. However, as time passed, that which seemed to be purely negative initiated changes which, at a later date, produced great blessings for us or for others. No amount of mental effort could have led us to contemplate these positive outcomes. The situations which seemed so negative, could only be turned over to God in trust, as our mental focus and energy were turned to more positive or useful pursuits.

When we focus on the negative, we must carefully examine why we are doing this. The goal of all our thoughts, all our actions, and all our conversation, should be to discover God's grace and to share that grace with others. If you are mentally dwelling on something that is not serving that purpose, you need to change your mental focus. Think about, and talk about, something you regard as a blessing. Concentrate on those things where you can see God and his grace making a difference in your life and the lives of others. In general, we need to follow the advice of Scripture that is reflected in a song by Johnny Mercer and Harold Arlen:

> *"You've got to accentuate the positive ~ Eliminate the negative ~ Latch on to the affirmative ~ Don't mess with Mister In-Between."*

The positive results of this change in mental focus are reflected in a story of a woman whose life was filled with tragedy. To the amazement of her friends she maintained an extremely positive outlook on life. Her example often inspired others to move forward in life when they faced seemingly insurmountable challenges. When asked what her secret was, she responded:

> *"When I go to bed, I begin my prayers to God with thanksgiving for every single blessing he has given me that day. I make sure that I list every blessing he has given. By the time I'm done with that I'm just too exhausted to talk about my problems, so I just commend those to his care and go to sleep."*

The secret revealed in this story shouldn't be a secret to Christians. St. Paul tells us (Php 4:6-7) *"Do not be anxious about anything, but in everything, by prayer and petition, with thanksgiving, present your requests to God. And the peace of God, which transcends all understanding, will guard your hearts and your minds in Christ Jesus."*

When you find yourself dwelling on negative events in your private thoughts or in your discussions with others, you need to ask yourself why. If your mental preoccupation or discussion is not focused on how you might bring God's grace to bear on a problem, you need to move on in your thinking or the topic of discussion. Let God worry about those things where you can't immediately see how his grace is at work. Focus on areas where you can see his grace at work or where you think you can be his agent for sharing that grace with the world.

Study and Discuss

Find someone to talk about the positives in your life and in theirs (Waking up and not finding your name in the obituary notices does not count as a positive).

1) **List at least 3 positive events or facts about your childhood.**

2) **List at least 3 positive moments from the last week.**

3) **List at least 3 positive moments from today.**

When you are feeling depressed, find some activity that helps you change your focus. Recite a psalm of praise. Think or talk about something good that happened recently. Ask someone else to tell you about the good things that are happening in their life. Think about ways that you can lift up and encourage others. If nothing else comes to mind, share a good joke with a friend.

If you aren't focused on how God has been gracious, how he will be gracious, or how his grace can help others, your focus needs to change.

What Do We Do with Praise?

One of the experiments described in an earlier lesson dealt with a group of people who were given three bogus personality evaluations: one positive, one neutral, and one negative. When asked which of the evaluators they would like to meet, depressed people showed a strong desire to meet with the negative evaluator. Those who were not depressed showed a strong desire to meet with the positive evaluator.

This experiment, and many others, demonstrates that the focus of the human mind is strongly impacted by mood. Left unchecked, this tendency forces the depressed mind deeper into depression by discounting positive events. Given the choice between listening to a positive evaluation or a negative evaluation, the depressed person will "disqualify" the positive and "emphasize" the negative. In the case of extreme anxiety, when good things are happening, the anxious person will spend their time pondering what will upset the apple cart, rather than simply rejoicing in what is good. We review this cognitive distortion:

4. DISQUALIFYING THE POSITIVE

You reject positive experiences by insisting they "don't count" for some reason or other. In this way you can maintain a negative belief that is contradicted by your everyday experiences.

Examples

a. *You studied hard for a test and got the highest grade in the class. Your instructor pulls you aside and says, "I can see from your test that you have a real grasp of this material." You respond by saying, "No, I'm just a good guesser."*

b. *You just had a professional portrait taken. Someone tells you that you look beautiful and you respond by saying, "No, the photographer is just really good at touching up stuff!" or someone tells you that you look great in a certain dress and you respond, "Yeah, it hides the fat well."*

c. *Someone evaluates a project you have been working on very positively. When a friend asks you how your evaluation went you tell them the evaluator's response but then qualify it by saying, "I think they were just trying to be nice to me."*

In this form of thinking individuals tend to take clearly positive events and find a way to put a negative spin to them. These thoughts arise from a self-belief that we are not worthy of good things, often identified as low-self esteem. People caught up in this thinking style can actually feel guilty about feeling good.

Self-image is generally established in our childhood. Low self-image is particularly characteristic of children who have suffered from various forms of abuse. Though they do not talk about, or even deny their experiences, there is a lingering shame, guilt, or fear which colors their interpretation of all positive events in their life. Low self-image is also common among children who have experienced criticism for their appearance, such as children being overweight. Another interesting source of these feelings can be brought about by extreme praise.

In 1978, Pauline Clance and psychologist Suzanne Imes published a study entitled "The Impostor Phenomenon Among High Achieving Women." Our world sometimes overly compensates people for certain achievements especially in the entertainment and athletic fields. As people become increasingly successful, they experience a growing sense that the world hasn't figured out who they really are, and that once the world does figure this out, they will be rejected.

In this study Clance and Imes found that women experiencing the "Impostor Phenomenon" came from two distinct backgrounds. One group of women had a sibling who was designated the "intelligent" member of the family, while they had been told they were the "sensitive" or "socially adept" one. The implication from the family was that this person could never compete with the other sibling no matter what they accomplished. In the second group of women there was a completely different family dynamic.

The family conveys to the girl that she is superior in every way – intellect, personality, appearance, and talents. There is nothing that she cannot do if she wants to, and she can do it with ease. . . . In the family members' eyes she is perfect. The child, however, begins to have experiences in which she cannot do any and everything she wants to. She does have difficulty in achieving certain things. Yet she feels obligated to fulfill expectations of her family, even though she knows she cannot keep up the act forever. Because she is so indiscriminately praised for everything, she begins to distrust her parents' perceptions of her. Moreover, she begins to doubt herself.[63]

Psychotherapists try to help these people accept the praise of others and stop dismissing their gifts or talents as unworthy. By contrast, a Scriptural approach to this problem begins with recognizing the truth about our human nature: Because of our sin we don't deserve praise!

Though the apostle Paul achieved much for the sake of God's kingdom, he also realized he deserved nothing.

Study and Discuss

Read 1 Corinthians 15:9

Did Paul deserve to be called an apostle?

Read 1 Timothy 1:14-16

With 1 being very bad and 10 being very good, where would Paul place himself on a "goodness" scale?

Why would God pick Paul to be his servant?

Read Romans 7:14-25

What happens when Paul tries to do something good?

---

[63]Clance and Imes, "The Impostor Phenomenon Among High Achieving Women" (Psychotherapy Theory, Research and Practice Volume 15, #3, Fall 1978) p. 3

Scripturally speaking, we don't deserve anything positive. On the contrary, we deserve nothing but eternal death and hell. Even in the best of humanity, there are huge flaws. Even in our best efforts, there are mistakes and less than good intentions. An example of this is revealed in the life Mother Teresa, a Catholic Nun on the way to sainthood.

Mother Teresa has long been noted as a model of compassion, sacrificial living, and a deep faith in God. After her death in September of 1997, the Roman Catholic Church seemed destined to elevate her status to that of a saint. The obligatory investigation into her life, as a prelude to sainthood, revealed that the faith of this supposed saint was not as noble as most people thought.

In her diaries Mother Teresa wrote, *"In my own soul, I feel the terrible pain of this loss. I feel that God does not want me, that God is not God and that he does not really exist."*[64] Such thoughts seem out of place from someone who, on the outside, seemed like a person of great faith. Elsewhere Mother Teresa wrote that because she was *"forever smiling,"* people thought *"my faith, my hope and my love are overflowing and that my intimacy with God and union with his will fill my heart. If only they knew . . . "* The energetic, selfless, over achieving Mother Teresa that everyone saw on the outside, appears from her diaries to have been, at times, a very depressed person on the inside.

Depressed people are often over-achievers because of their quest to satisfy that nagging doubt, "Am I worthy?" The psychological approach to that question would be to affirm that we are worthy. The Scriptural approach to that question is to affirm that we are not worthy, and can never become worthy. However, our unworthiness is not an excuse to disqualify the positive things that happen in our life.

Christians affirm the positive in their lives as gifts of God's grace. We are not worthy of the good things that happen to us, but we are thankful for every blessing. While any praise we receive should always be forwarded to God, to simply disqualify or discount praise offered to us, is actually to disqualify and diminish the grace of God at work in our

---

[64]Bruce Johnston, "Mother Teresa's diary reveals her crisis of faith" (Telegraph.co.uk NEWS, 11/29/2002)

lives. Rather than discounting that work, God encourages us to give thanks for his grace and tell about his goodness to others.

Study and Discuss

Read 1 Thessalonians 5:18; Colossians 3:17; and Ephesians 5:19-20

When should we be thankful to God?

Reflecting upon our worthiness is a fruitless endeavor when considering the blessings we receive in life. Rather, the dominant question for the Christian is how we can use the blessings that God has given us to reflect to others the glory of his grace. Thus, the apostle Paul, in the passage from 1 Timothy quoted earlier, uses his selection as an apostle to reflect to others how gracious God is.

Study and Discuss

Read Jeremiah 9:23-24; Galatians 6:14; and 1 Corinthians 1:27-31

What should Christians boast about?

The only thing that was ever pure in this world after the fall into sin was Jesus Christ. After the fall, every word, thought and action of mankind is always tainted by sin in some way.

If someone compliments you and you think that there may be some ulterior motive at play, you may be right. If you experience some positive reward in your life, you can always think of some reason why you are not fully worthy of what you have received. If you find someone who loves you, their love won't be perfect and you won't be fully worthy of that love. This is our reality as sinners, but it is not the reality God would have us dwell upon.

When we encounter the positive, God would simply have us give thanks for it. Be thankful for the grace we don't deserve. Rejoice in the grace of God which brings blessings to us even through less than pure and less than perfect means. Yes we don't deserve it, but this points out even more beautifully the wonder of God's grace to us. Paul writes in 2 Corinthians 4:7, *"But we have this treasure in jars of clay to show that this all-surpassing power is from God and not from us."*

Lesson 7 ~ Weekly Activities

Identifying and Attacking Mental Filters

Pick an extended period of your life from which you remember few, if any, positive experiences. Write at least a 500 word essay describing "only" the good things that happened to you in this period of life.

Analyzing Cognitive Distortions

Continue to write down and analyze one cognitive distortion each day. It is important for you to continue to examine your thinking styles so that you can better recognize distorted, negative thinking, and replace it with gospel centered positive thinking. Use the Law ~ Gospel Thinking Cards to help you identify these distortions and to try and identify gospel centered alternatives.

Caring for the Body and Spirit God Gave me

Do not neglect your body as we focus on mind and spirit issues. Continue to monitor and improve your diet, exercise, and sleep regimen. Continue to discuss your progress with others, and evaluate how changes in your activities (spending time talking, playing music, reading, or adding other activities to your day) are affecting your overall mood.

Scripture Reading

For your daily reading you are encouraged to read the entire book of Exodus (yes, it's a bit longer than the other readings). While reading the book of Exodus, think about the many ways that Israel allowed their own feelings and agendas to cloud their interpretation and reaction to God's actions. In addition, include the following supplemental readings on the recommended day and answer the associated questions.

Day 2 ~ Read Mark 4:34 - 41

How did the disciples interpret Jesus' act of sleeping in the boat while the storm was raging?

From a worldly (non-faith) point of view, were their fears and interpretation of Jesus' actions rational?

Why was Jesus disappointed with the reaction of his disciples?

Day 4 ~ Read Exodus 16:1-16

What false interpretation of events did the Israelites apply to Moses and to God when they were hungry?

How did God respond?

Read Exodus 17:1-7

What false interpretation of events did the Israelites apply to Moses and to God when they were thirsty?

How did God respond?

Day 6 ~ Read Numbers 21:1-9

What mighty act does God perform for the Israelites?

How long do the Israelites remember this mighty act?

What act of punishment does God inflict upon Israel?

Did God offer Israel a way of being saved from this punishment?

What was the purpose of God punishing Israel in this way?

- NOTES -

- NOTES -

Lesson 8

The Distortions of "Jumping to Conclusions" Through "Mind Reading" or "Negative Prediction"

What's the Point? *Using the false belief that we can read minds or predict the future we "jump to conclusions" that push us into depression. Here we focus on the promises of God that set our minds at ease knowing that our future is in his loving hands.*

The first temptation in the Garden of Eden dealt with man trying to acquire knowledge that only God has. Satan enticed Adam and Eve to seek this knowledge by lying about God's character. Satan told Adam and Eve that God had lied when he said they would die if they ate fruit from the tree of the knowledge of good and evil.

According to Satan, God lied because he wanted power only for himself (Gn 3:5). *"For God knows that when you eat of it your eyes will be opened, and you will be like God, knowing good and evil."* Satan lied! He lied about God's character, and he lied about our ability to play God.

God has certain qualities that we can never possess. While we can only know the outward appearance of people, Scripture tells us that God can go beyond outward appearance (1Sa 16:7). God knows (Ps 44:21) *"the secrets of our hearts."* God also tells us that he has the unique ability to foretell what the future will be (Is 44:6-8). God has knowledge that we don't have, and can never have. However, as Adam and Eve demonstrated, that doesn't stop us from trying to play God.

When we try to play God, the results are usually negative. Nevertheless, from Adam and Eve's first sin until now, people continue this vain attempt. We play God by trying to read the minds of others and by trying to predict what the future will bring. These cognitive distortions, which we identify as "jumping to conclusions," are rooted in our inability to trust in God when he says that he will care for us.

5. JUMPING TO CONCLUSIONS

You make a negative interpretation even though there are no definite facts that convincingly support your conclusion.

CAN WE READ MINDS?

The first form of "jumping to conclusions" rests on the false assumption that we can look into the minds and hearts of others and tell what they are thinking. All of us do this from time to time. Some people exhibit a reasonable ability to guess at what people are thinking based upon outward clues or experience. Of course, even the best observers of human nature are sometimes wrong. Even mechanical lie detectors can be fooled.

When caught up in depression this human tendency to try and read minds is no longer based upon a reasonable guess from the outward clues others may give us. In the grips of depression, even our previous experiences with a person become a false guide to what they might be thinking.

The depressed mind has a biased image of past experiences. Past positive experiences tend to be forgotten, while past negative experiences are over-generalized. Positive encounters from the past may be discounted as a new interpretation is placed over them. Thus, even our past experience with an individual ceases to be a realistic guide to what a person might be thinking, making us even less capable of accurately reading someone's mind. To review this form of "jumping to conclusions":

A. MIND READING

You arbitrarily conclude that someone is reacting negatively to you, and you don't bother to check this out.

a. *You walk in a room and see a group of people whispering. You are convinced that they are talking negatively about you.*

b. *You have a conflict with your family or a group of close friends. You cut off the conversation that would lead to a resolution by exclaiming, "You all hate me!" and leave the room.*

c. *You are at a restaurant waiting for a date to show up who is 10 minutes late. This person seemed very excited about going out with you. You assume you did something wrong and have been stood up. You leave the restaurant as your date sits frustrated in a traffic jam.*

In the depths of depression the thoughts of others are presumed to be "guilty until proven innocent." Even positive events can be twisted by the depressed mind reader into a negative incident by questioning the motives and attitudes of others.

For instance, someone compliments you and you presume that their motive is to manipulate you into doing something. Because you don't believe there was a positive motive, you question the person making the compliment. "You're not saying that just to be nice! What are you trying to get out of me?"

As the depressed person responds to others based upon their false assumptions, their response has the effect of becoming a self-fulfilling prophecy. When the motive for a compliment is called into question, the person who made the compliment may now respond with a criticism such as: "You just can't take a compliment, can you?" The observation is correct, but its negative tone tends to confirm the depressed individual's first assumption; namely, that the person making the compliment had some negative motive. The only thing that will be remembered from this exchange is the criticism, not the compliment.

As we analyze "mind reading" it is important to understand why we try to do it. Simply put, we want to read the minds of others to help guide our own behavior. If we can respond to others based upon what they are thinking, we believe that we can gain a manipulative advantage in our relationships. Imagine the advantage a batter would have if he could read a pitcher's mind!

While we believe that knowing the thoughts of others gives us more control over our life, the exact opposite is the actual result. When our behavior is linked to the opinions of others, we have lost control of the decision making process in our life. We have enslaved our actions to the presumed ideas and opinions of others. Instead of living a life of action, our lives become a constant reaction to the thoughts of others.

Even when people are great guessers at the motivations or thoughts of others, this is not a healthy way to live your life. Even at its best, the life of a mind reader is ruled by the whims and ever-changing attitudes of others, rather than a consistent set of rules and promises made by a loving God. When the mind reader is someone trapped in depression, their life becomes ruled by a constant reaction to the ghosts and shadows of attitudes that have no basis in reality.

The negative way in which the depressed person imagines the thoughts of others provides justification for withdrawal from social and work activities. Negative perceptions inspire over reaction to the slightest criticism. Genuine offers of help are twisted into an attempt to make the depressed person look foolish or inferior.

The constant negative interpretation of positive actions frustrates and angers those around the depressed person. As the frustration and anger of friends, family, and co-workers begins to reveal itself, the depressed person believes they have now received objective confirmation of what they have believed all along. The depressed person doesn't recognize that they are generating these negative feelings in others by their own false assumptions and false accusations.

The Christian can avoid the trap of mind reading because the Christian's life is not rooted in a reaction to the thoughts and ideas of other sinners. The Christian life is dictated by the words and gracious promises of God, regardless of what others may think.

Study and Discuss

Read Galatians 1:8-10; 2:5-6 and 1 Thessalonians 2:4

What governed the way the apostle Paul behaved?

Read 1 Corinthians 4:3-5

What weight does Paul place upon the judgments of others in determining his behavior?

Though not specifically stated, why do you think Paul is not afraid of the Lord's judgment, even though he is "not innocent?"

Study and Discuss

Read 1 John 3:13-20

What impact should the world "hating" us have on our Christian behavior?

What forms the basis of our love for others?

In combating depression it is vitally important to evaluate the extent to which our actions are based upon the attitudes of others (whether real or imagined), and to substitute actions rooted in God's love for us and his love for others. In essence, the goal is to trade in hundreds of gods for one God in our life. The great thing about serving this one God, is that even when we do fail him, he forgives us. Even if our own hearts condemn us, we can be at peace because God is greater than our own hearts. Through Jesus, all condemnation has been removed.

While the Christian life is focused on pleasing God rather than pleasing people, the Christian is not totally oblivious to what others think. While Christian behavior is not a reaction to the thoughts and attitudes of others, Christians do try to influence how others think in fulfillment of the mission God has given us.

Study and Discuss

Read Romans 12:19-21 and Proverbs 20:22

Why is "revenge" a non-issue for Christians?

How does the Christian deal with evil and why?

Read Titus 2:9-10

Why should slaves try to please their masters?

For the depressed person the thoughts and attitudes of others, real or imagined, serve as a justification for withdrawal, anger, or vengeful behavior. Even when these thoughts start out as imagined, they can become a self-fulfilling prophecy as social and family contacts become frustrated with the constant questioning of motive or the angry reactions they receive after good intentioned acts of help and advice.

For the Christian, God's will and grace are the sole guide and motivation for living. Life is not a reaction to what others are doing. Rather, life becomes an action focused on bringing God's love and grace to others.

Do We Need to Know the Future?

The second form of "jumping to conclusions" rests on the false assumption that we can predict the consequences or results of every action. Again, all of us do this from time to time. Some people are reasonably adept at evaluating the consequences of any specific action, especially in areas of life where they have a wealth of experience to look back upon. However, during depression these conclusions are not based on a reasonable assessment of the facts. Instead, they are based on our own negative outlook.

B. NEGATIVE PREDICTION

You can anticipate that things will turn out badly, and you feel convinced that your prediction is an already-established fact.

Examples

a. *You are having pain but won't go and see the doctor because you know that he is going to tell you that you have a cancer tumor and you will die soon. Why bother the doctor?*

b. *You know that you are going to fail a test so you won't waste your time studying.*

c. *You had a misunderstanding with a friend, but you refuse to talk to them and try to correct the misinformation because you know that they won't change their mind.*

In this cognitive distortion, individuals look at future events and circumstances in their life presuming that all roads lead to defeat or a negative experience. In learning situations, depressed people say things such as “I’ll never get it!” or “I’ll never be good at it!” When facing new social settings they say “Nobody will like me!” or “I won’t fit in!”

The future of people who employ negative prediction is without hope. In this hopeless state they avoid trying new things, learning new skills, meeting new people, and even seeking help for their condition because “it’s not going to do any good!”

Sometimes this negative outlook on the future may be rooted in a life filled with failures. These failures can be the result of our own self-fulfilling actions, or simply the result of the circumstances we find ourselves in. An over-critical parent may train their child to anticipate a negative result from anything they try to do.

Sometimes a pattern of negative prediction arises from one failure that, in an individual’s mind, has come to define their entire life. Even though this individual could point to a number of successful events in their life, one event becomes the sole measure of their ability to succeed.

In secular CBT this type of thinking will be modified by pointing out and focusing on all the positive things we can do. People may be instructed to tackle small projects or behaviors that build a legacy of success. From that foundation the individual is then encouraged to be more daring, from their perspective, to the point where they do not see all new endeavors in their life as a new opportunity to fail miserably.

These techniques may be successful in changing our emotional outlook, but there are some scriptural and life realities that these behavioral techniques fail to address. One of the realities that is ignored in this technique is the fact that ultimately, all our worldly efforts do result in failure. The author of Ecclesiastes dramatically and repeatedly points out this fact of life.

Many interpreters of Ecclesiastes see this book of Scripture as a fatalistic, depressed outlook upon the world. Solomon, however, is simply taking a look at the results of our life apart from a belief in eternity. Solomon clues the reader in that he is talking about a limited world view by the use of the phrase “under the sun”; that is, looking at life from a purely worldly perspective. Solomon uses this phrase 29 times throughout the book of Ecclesiastes.

Study and Discuss

Read Ecclesiastes 2:17-23; 5:12-17

What do we get for all our human efforts?

From Solomon, one of wisest people that ever lived, we learn the true reality of life. Whatever you accomplish in life will be forgotten in one or two generations. Wealth you accumulate in life will probably be wasted by your heirs. If you work really hard so that you can relax and enjoy your retirement, you'll probably have a heart attack and die the week after you stop working. Righteous people often get what the evil deserve and evil people often get what the righteous deserve. People don't listen to the wise but instead they follow fools. These aren't negative predictions, they are simply the depressing reality of life in a sinful world.

The point that Solomon makes throughout Ecclesiastes, which many readers miss, is that life can be enjoyed despite these depressing realities. Solomon, however, sees this happening only for the person who changes his focus from worldly accomplishments, to pleasing God. Not life "under the sun," but life "under the Son."

Study and Discuss

Read Ecclesiastes 12:12-14

What is the "bottom line" of what we should be doing during our life on this earth?

Risking an oversimplification of Solomon's message, God is not outcome oriented, but process oriented. What we accomplish in this world will ultimately be destroyed when Christ comes again. However, our relationship with God, built upon his grace and love toward us, will endure for eternity. That relationship is all that ultimately matters.

Overcoming negative prediction involves switching our focus from outcome to process, as well as a radical redefinition of success. One of the chief problems with a secular CBT approach to negative prediction is that it is fundamentally rooted in our efforts and accomplishments.

Study and Discuss

Read John 15:5-6

Without Christ, what can we accomplish?

With Christ, what can we accomplish?

Read Philippians 4:10-13

In what situations can the apostle Paul be content?

What is Paul's secret to contentment?

Christians recognize that whatever we do apart from Christ is destined for failure. Our focus should be on that which Christ can do in us and through us. This change in focus forces us to find a new definition of success.

Study and Discuss

Read Ephesians 1:7-10

What is God's ultimate purpose for the world?

Read Matthew 28:18-20

What is the goal of Christ's authority?

The Christian life is focused on sharing Christ. This goal is not only accomplished through our strengths, but also through our weakness. We can share Christ not only in our successes, but also in our failures.

Study and Discuss

Read 1 Corinthians 1:25-31

What kind of people are God's first choice in witnessing to this world?

What does it mean to be a success in God's eyes? A successful person in God's eyes is one who simply shares God's love with others at every opportunity. The worldly skills we have, the worldly honor we may receive, the material blessings we are able to accumulate, are of little consequence in measuring godly success. As Paul points out in reference from 1 Corinthians, worldly success is frequently counter productive to our success as a Christian witness.

Study and Discuss

Read Matthew 5:1-12

Would you consider the "blessed" people in these passages "successful" from this world's viewpoint?

It is easy in this world to predict the negative, but those predictions should have nothing to do with how we live out our lives. What we do for Christ may not always be considered successful as measured by this world, but anything, even our weaknesses, can be successfully used by God to bear witness to Christ. In everything God is working to bring eternal blessings to ourselves and others, and in the end, nothing else really matters. Jesus tells us:

(Mt 6:19-21), *"Do not store up for yourselves treasures on earth, where moth and rust destroy, and where thieves break in and steal. But store up for yourselves treasures in heaven, where moth and rust do not destroy, and where thieves do not break in and steal. For where your treasure is, there your heart will be also."*

Our job is to tell others about Christ and what he has accomplished for us. However, we often lose this focus even in the way we describe Christ to others.

Frequently, Christians become overly focused on prophecy and concerns regarding the second coming of Christ. Instead of talking about what Christ has done for us, the focus of our witness becomes what Christ will do to us if we don't shape up. The Christian message is changed from good news to bad news. Our witness to Christ is filled with "negative prediction."

Jesus never wanted his second coming to be the focus of our Christian witness. When Jesus does speak about the end times, he tells us:

(Mt 24:4-36) *"Watch out that no one deceives you. For many will come in my name, claiming, 'I am the Christ, ' and will deceive many. . . this gospel of the kingdom will be preached in the whole world as a testimony to all nations, and then the end will come. . . if anyone says to you, 'Look, here is the Christ!' or, 'There he is!' do not believe it. . . See, I have told you ahead of time. So if anyone tells you, 'There he is, out in the desert,' do not go out; or, 'Here he is, in the inner rooms,' do not believe it. . . Heaven and earth will pass away, but my words will never pass away. No one knows about that day or hour, not even the angels in heaven, nor the Son, but only the Father."*

Christians are not supposed to focus on when Christ will come again, but on preaching *"the gospel of the kingdom."* The end of the world won't come until that work is finished. The apostle Paul writes, (1 Co 2:2) *"For I resolved to know nothing while I was with you except Jesus Christ and him crucified."*

Christ wants us to have an eternal perspective on life rooted in what he accomplished for us on the cross. Who cares if the world might end tomorrow? The only question that should matter for us is how we can share the good news today.

As we keep our focus on the gospel, our definition of success is changed along with our means of measuring it. Predicting an earthly outcome for anything we do, or even trying to predict the end of the world, becomes a somewhat meaningless exercise. The primary question for the Christian is not "What will happen?" but "How can I use what has happened to bear witness to Christ?" "How will God use this event to build myself or others up in Christ?"

The Christian gives up trying to predict the future because the Christian trusts that the future is in the hands of a loving and merciful God. A spiritual outlook based on this trust, together with a redefinition of our purpose in life that is rooted in God's loving and gracious plan, is the ultimate key to defeating the cognitive distortion of negative prediction.

Lesson 8 ~ Weekly Activities

Reviewing Cognitive Distortions

Continue to examine your thinking styles using the tools located in the appendix so that you can better recognize distorted, negative thinking, and replace it with gospel centered positive thinking. Use the Law ~ Gospel Thinking Cards to help you identify these distortions and to find gospel centered alternatives to ways you have been thinking.

Caring for the Body and Spirit God Gave me

Remember that you are body, mind, and spirit and do not neglect your body as we focus on mind and spirit issues. Continue to track your sleep, diet, and exercise routines. Discuss your progress with your support partner. Talk about your other life style changes such as spending more time talking, playing music, or adding other activities to your day.

Scripture Reading

This week you are encouraged to read the entire book of Ecclesiastes for your daily reading (roughly two chapters per day). It is important as you read this letter to remember that whenever Solomon uses the phrase "under the Sun," he is referring to life apart from knowledge of God and his grace.

The fundamental message of Ecclesiastes is that without God and his eternal hope, life is ultimately meaningless. However, joy and fulfillment can still be found in a life centered in God. The readings given below emphasize the fact that our future is secure in God, and that we don't have to worry about our future.

Day 2 ~ Read Psalm 121

What promises does God make regarding our future?

What qualities or traits does God possess that allow him to make these kinds of promises?

DAY 4 ~ Read Psalm 23

Looking at this Psalm, describe what the life of a sheep is like without a shepherd leading it?

Does having the Lord as our shepherd mean we will not pass through dark valleys?

How does having the Lord as our shepherd change our outlook on the future?

DAY 6 ~ Read Genesis 22:1-14 and Hebrews 11:10-19

Without the perspective of the resurrection, what would have happened to God's promise to Abraham if Isaac had died?

How did Abraham's relationship with God enable him to contemplate killing his only son?

Based on the name Abraham gave to this mountain (Gn 22:14), what did God prove to Abraham through this event?

- NOTES -

- NOTES -

Lesson 9

The Distortions of "Magnification" or "Minimization" and "Emotional Reasoning"

What's the Point? *Frequently fears and anxieties drive us to set aside a realistic assessment of life, allowing the cognitive distortions of "magnification or minimization" or "emotional reasoning" to paint a depressing portrait of our world. These distortions need to be replaced with the objective truth of the promises that God makes to us in his gracious word.*

WHAT MAKES SOMETHING IMPORTANT?

6. MAGNIFICATION OR MINIMIZATION

You exaggerate the importance of things (such as your goof-up or someone else's achievement), or you inappropriately shrink things until they appear tiny (your good qualities or the imperfections of others).

Examples

a. *You get a pimple on your face just before a party and refuse to go because you know that everyone will be staring at you all night (magnification of your goof up).*

b. *You won't apply for a promotion because you know the other applicants. You know that you could never be as good as they are (magnification of the achievement of others and minimizing your qualities).*

c. *Your spouse just gave you a black eye in a fit of rage and you rationalize it by pointing to some failure on your part. Your child just called you every name in the book because you asked them to be home at a reasonable hour. You rationalize it by saying your child has always been over sensitive (minimizing the other person's imperfections).*

As pointed out in the section on "jumping to conclusions," the life of a Christian should be one of action, not reaction. Our actions are governed by the will and promises of God, not the whims of others or the outcome we might predict for our actions.

In combating the distortions of "magnification" or "minimization" secular CBT will encourage people to use a more logical and reasonable means of assessing the importance of events. The problem with this model is that in many areas of life logic and reason are not always clear cut guides to what matters the most or the least.

Is a break out of acne a good reason to cancel an appearance at a party? Would an acne breakout be a good reason to change an appointment for a class picture? Where is the line crossed between underestimating yourself, a reasonable assessment of your gifts and talents, and visions of grandiosity? When should you overlook the faults of others and when should you call attention to them?

Even Scripture does not give us a specific answer to every question in life. To do so would require a book larger than the Library of Congress. Yet, at the heart of these two cognitive distortions is a fundamentally spiritual question: Are we evaluating events from a spiritual state of peace or anxiety, joy or depression? This question will be addressed at greater length under "emotional reasoning," but it highlights how values are influenced by spiritual and emotional states.

If you just won the lottery, you just got engaged to the love of your life, and you just won an Olympic gold medal, finding out that someone just put a dent in your new car is probably not going to ruffle your feathers very much. You may feel a momentary flash of anger or sadness, but your mind is so overwhelmed with other fantastic things that you will likely brush this moment aside and carry on with more important concerns in life.

On the other hand, if you just filed for bankruptcy, your spouse just filed for divorce, and you just heard that you were cut from the roster of the local church softball team, a dent in your new car might cause an emotional explosion. Thoughts of taking a baseball bat to the perpetrator's car may race through your head (magnification), or you might leave your new car and take the bus home uttering something like "I don't care anymore! They've taken everything else! They can have this too!" (minimization).

The same event can prompt wildly different responses depending upon your emotional and spiritual state of mind. Thus, people who operate from a spiritual state where they regard themselves as worthless respond in an inappropriate way to the behavior of others. They tolerate fits of rage and abusive behavior. They make excuses for others even to the point of blaming themselves for the bad behavior of others.

People who operate from a spiritual state where they feel they have no control over life frequently over react to situations. Even the smallest inconvenience can cause emotional explosions.

In dealing with the cognitive distortions of "magnification" and "minimization" it is critical to identify what emotions are involved in our value system. Are we making value judgments based on fears, doubts, worries, or guilt, or are we making value judgments from a perspective of peace where we are confident our needs will be met, our future is secure, and our sins are forgiven?

Unfortunately, while we may reasonably and logically identify where our value system is based, changing a fearful or guilty heart, overcoming a sense of worthlessness or being out of control, cannot be accomplished by a mental trick or cognitive training. These are matters of the heart best addressed by the Holy Spirit as he works in us through the word of God. These are spiritual matters that can only be repaired through the spiritual tools God gives us.

Having identified what causes these cognitive distortions of "magnification" and "minimization" we will more fully address the issues we have raised here as we deal with "emotional reasoning." What we value cannot easily be separated from how we feel emotionally and spiritually.

Do My Feelings Matter?

While our brain functions as a comprehensive whole we have learned that certain parts of the brain carry out different functions. Emotions arise in a different part of the brain than logic. However, these two facets of thought are still interconnected. Memories, even impersonal facts, are interlaced with emotional content.

Earlier we discussed an experiment where students memorized 16 words after being placed in a specific mood. Upon returning the next day the students were then placed in a the same mood or the opposite mood. Their ability to recall what they memorized was directly related to whether they were experiencing the same mood as the day before.

Subconsciously most of what we know and think is interconnected to our emotions. As we learned in earlier lessons, emotional reactions are also faster than logical reactions. Emotional reasoning is the automatic reasoning we have when encountering a new situation.[65]

> *"Emotional reactions arise chiefly in a region of the brain called the limbic system, which is very fast-acting and can respond to events on the basis of quick-and-dirty impressions. This nimbleness of response has survival value in some situations — such as noticing a fast-moving object that could be a car or truck approaching as you cross a street."* . . .

> *"But on other occasions — such as complex situations where you need to call on more of your accumulated knowledge and experience, speed can be a disadvantage. The more complete information you need at such times has to be processed by the lateral prefrontal cortex of your brain — which gets into gear about half a second later than your limbic system. This short delay is often enough that your thinking, under the influence of an automated emotional reaction, heads off in a biased direction that you may come to regret."*

It is virtually impossible to separate emotions from the thinking process, but in certain circumstances emotions, particularly negative emotions, cease to be just a piece of the thinking puzzle. Instead, our negative emotions are allowed to paint the complete picture when it comes to the reasoning process. Examples of this can be found in the many "phobias" that exist.

Phobias are an extreme form of emotional reasoning. For instance, consider how a person prone to phobias would react to hearing news about someone who got stuck in an elevator and died. The fear this story generates, would drive this type of person to the decision that they will never ride in an elevator again.

---

[65]Bush, John Winston, PHD, "A fuller explanation of CBT" (Nov. 10, 2002, http://www.cognitivetherapy.com/fuller.html)

Suppose this person reads about a plane that crashed. The frightening details lead the person to conclude that they will never fly in a plane. The fact that more people injure themselves on stairs each year, or that per mile traveled, planes are much safer than riding in a car, plays no role in these kind of decisions. People with phobias have a perception of reality so dominated by emotion that logic and facts have no bearing on the decision making process.

As mentioned earlier, the brain of a person with a phobia has a hardwired neural path from, for instance, the image of a spider to the emotional center for fear. When the image of the spider appears the emotional center reacts, faster than the logic center, and because the emotional response is so intense logic is never brought to bear in considering how to respond to the spider.

Individuals can be sent screaming from a room with the full knowledge that they are being chased with a plastic spider or a plastic mouse. There is no rational basis for their response! Their thinking has become totally governed by the emotional center of the brain. Only with determined effort and repeated training can the person with such a phobia retrain their brain to approach such situations with a more reasoned response.

In depression, our interpretation and response to life becomes hard wired to the center for negative emotions. Since our emotional response to events is faster than our logical response, the further people sink into depression the more difficult it becomes for the brain to conceive of any other way of looking at life, no matter how unreasonable and illogical their perspective may seem to others.

7. EMOTIONAL REASONING

You assume that your negative emotions necessarily reflect the way things really are: "I feel it, therefore it must be true."

Examples

a. *An alcoholic family member who drifts from job to job just coerced you into lending them $500.00 that you really couldn't afford to lend. Other family members said you shouldn't do it, and you even had thoughts that this really wasn't going to help your alcoholic family member, but you were made to feel so guilty that you did it anyway.*

b. You are always angry because everybody around you is always trying to mess up your life.

c. Everyone at work tells you that you are working too hard. Yet, you refuse to take vacation time and go into work even when you are seriously ill because you are worried that someone might do your job better and you will be replaced.

As depression deepens, people tend to assign infallibility to their feelings. Feelings dictate every action despite all facts to the contrary. This depressed emotional state also influences our memories of the past, casting a dark shadow on what once were regarded as positive times in our lives.

A 1982 study[66] on the effects of mood and memory showed that when depressed people recall their childhoods *"they are more likely to recall an unhappy, deprived childhood; after their depression passes, they recall a far rosier childhood."* College students who were put into a particular mood through the use of music and talking about either happy or sad events were asked to write down what happened in their lives over the last two weeks. Students, who were randomly put into a sad mood, recalled predominantly unhappy events. Students, who were randomly put into a happy mood, recalled predominantly happy events.

In the depressed person negative emotional reasoning colors every facet of life, and actually leads us to make choices that will further deepen the depression. These behaviors are called "mood congruent behaviors." The idea behind the big word is that "people will tend to dwell on, or even prefer, situations, people and things that confirm their current feelings."[67]

As discussed in earlier lessons, experiments tend to confirm the following behaviors. The experiments were typically performed on college students who were made to feel happy or sad, and then asked to describe or carry out certain activities or plans.

---

[66] Eich, E., & Metcalfe, J. (1989). "Mood dependent memory for internal versus external events." (Journal of Experimental Psychology: Learning, Memory and Cognition, 15, 443-455) found at http://www.cognitivetherapy.com/bower.html

[67] Bower, Gordon H. ~ Prof. of Psych. At Stanford Un. "Emotion and social judgments", Sept. 1995 found at http://www.cognitivetherapy.com/bower.html, Sept. 2003

1. Sad people cannot think of very many activities that they consider to be "pleasant."
2. When people are made temporarily sad, they lose interest in socializing, and find other people far less rewarding or attractive than do people who are not sad.
3. Depressed people tend to seek out more information about sad, unfortunate people than about happy people. When forced to socialize, depressed people prefer to meet and become better acquainted with unfortunate, unhappy people rather than with happy people.

In cognitive therapy a great deal of effort is spent in examining the basis for our reasoning process in an attempt to separate emotion from fact. People going through this form of therapy spend time with the therapist, and on their own, writing down and dissecting their thoughts, separating fact from emotion, then adjusting their behavior accordingly. It is hard work because our emotional responses physiologically occur before, and thus set the agenda for, our logical responses.

Secular cognitive therapists not only have to deal with depressed emotions taking over the reasoning process, but on occasion also work with people who have an overly positive view of life that does not reflect reality. The experiments mentioned earlier showed virtually identical, although inverted, rates of responses for happy and sad people in the choices they made. In other words the experiments showed that happiness influenced choices just as much as did sadness, but it did not evaluate whether those were the most appropriate or logical choices. In "manic depression" over optimism can be as dangerous as pessimism.

In sorting out the reasoning process Christians need to envision the battle line as not simply between emotion and reason, but spirit and flesh, Christ and Satan. Our decision making process is not only rooted in earthly facts, but the promises God makes to us in Christ Jesus. Christian decision making is not guided by reason or emotion, but by faith and the objective word of God, which will sometimes defy both our emotions and our logic.

I experienced a classic example of this conflict while serving in a summer chaplaincy program. The hospital was a cancer clinic, and the individual I was visiting was an active Christian who was overwhelmed with fear. This individual feared an upcoming surgery that was life threatening, but the focal point of her fear was not dying. The focal point of fear was her eternal destiny. This active Christian had convinced herself that she would wake up in hell if she died. Her emotional reasoning went like this.

1) I'm afraid I might die while being operated on.
2) Christians are not supposed to be afraid of dying.
3) Because I'm afraid my faith must be very weak.
4) I wonder if I'm really a Christian?
5) Maybe I won't go to heaven when I die!
6) Now I'm even more afraid that I might die!
7) Go back to step number 2

This individual's mind kept on recycling through steps 2-7 until she had reached a panic state. She was certain that she would wake up in hell if she died. Surprisingly, when asked if she believed that Jesus Christ paid for her sins when he died on the cross, this woman's answer was a very definite "Yes!" After this response the following Bible passages were read to her.

Study and Discuss

Read Romans 10:9-13 and Acts 2:38

What objective truth do these Bible passages teach about who will be saved?

Based on these Bible passages and her confession of Christ, where would this woman go if she died?

This personal experience is cited to demonstrate how emotional reasoning can color our understanding of our own personal salvation, as well as our ability to recall and interpret Scripture. This particular individual was an active Christian with years of Sunday school teaching experience. She was familiar with the Bible passages that ultimately calmed her fears, but in her distress her mental focus had become only those passages of Scripture which address the need for faith.

In evaluating her personal salvation, this person was ignoring the passages of Scripture that describe the content of true faith. She had become focused on what she must "do" (law), rather than what God has "done" (Gospel). She had turned faith into an action we must do for God, rather than an action by which we recognize what God has done for us. She had forgotten that faith itself is a gift, that faith the size of a mustard seed moves mountains. She needed to recall how God graciously answered the prayer of an anxious father, (Mk 9:24) *"I do believe; help me overcome my unbelief!"*

An important aspect of scriptural truth that this woman had ignored, and which many Christians fail to recognize, is the Bible's description of our dual character. She had forgotten that, while on earth, the Christian is both believer and unbeliever, saint and sinner.

Until we die the Christian always hears two voices calling from within. One voice is the Holy Spirit who calls to us with the words and promises of Scripture. The other voice is our old Adam, our sinful self, who is in bondage to Satan.

The fact that fears and doubts exist within each Christian heart should not be surprising, but expected. The critical issue for the Christian is not whether we have fears, doubts, guilt and worry, but whether we believe and trust in them or the promises that God has made to us. Do we act from our fears or from our faith?

Life is a constant battle of choices between the Spirit living within us, and our sinful nature. The problem for us is that the sinful nature is our natural self. When we are born into this world, we are spiritually dead. Our "automatic" response system is the sinful nature.

Study and Discuss

Read Romans 7:21-25; 8:5-11

How many minds live inside of the Christian?

What are the two minds or spirits?

What does the sinful nature (flesh) always want to do?

What does the Spirit of Christ always want to do?

The Christian always exists in a state of battle between the spirit and the sinful flesh. Peter's relationship with Christ provides a clear example of this battle. Peter is called "blessed" by Jesus for confessing (Mt 16:16) *"You are the Christ, the Son of the living God."* Just a few verses later, when Peter opposes Christ's death, he is told (Mt 16:23) *"Get behind me, Satan! You are a stumbling block to me; you do not have in mind the things of God, but the things of men."*

Are we blessed by Jesus or are we possessed by Satan? Are we a saint or a sinner? The biblical answer to the Christian is "Yes!" We are both until the day we die. The challenge for the Christian is to live and listen to the spirit. Live life based on promises of God rather than our negative emotions such as fear, doubt, worry, or guilt. When our life is ruled by these negative thoughts, Scripture describes our life as slavery: a behavior of obligation rather than a behavior of free choice.

Study and Discuss

Read John 8:31-34 and Romans 8:13-16

What is life lived in sin?

What is life lived in the spirit?

Sin is a response to guilt, fear, worry, doubt, and other negative emotions. Even when we are able to justify these emotions with reason and logic, they still should not be the motivation for a Christian's response to the world.

Study and Discuss

Read 1 John 4:15-19

What is perfect love and where does it come from?

Should fear be a part of our response to the world?

In "Gospel Therapy" the challenge is not to replace emotion with logic, but to replace both emotion and logic with faith in the promises God makes to us in the gospel. Doing this is neither natural nor easy. In our natural sinful state the gospel is completely foreign to us.

In Lesson 4, for instance, the question was asked, "Why should the Christian not steal?" The automatic response of virtually all people, including Christians, is something to the effect "It's wrong," "God forbids it," "It hurts other people" and the like. Fear of punishment or fear of guilt, essentially a negative emotional response, is the driving force restraining this type of behavior.

A witness to the ineffectiveness of fear as a control for our moral judgment is the widespread looting that often occurs when civil authority is absent or crippled in its ability to respond. A sad example of this was the city of New York during its 1977 power outage, or the city of New Orleans after hurricane Katrina.

What would you do if you knew you could get away with it? Behavior rooted in fear or driven by guilt has no solid foundation. It changes the moment the threat is removed. Christian behavior, as 1 John 4 points out, is not rooted in the negative emotion of fear but in a positive response to God's love for us in Christ. The apostle Paul tells us that the righteous (Rm 1:17) *"live by faith"* and that (Rm 6:14) *"sin shall not be your master, because you are not under law, but under grace."*

Our natural inclination in responding to the world is to focus on "What will I do?" Enlightened by the gospel, the Christian learns to first ask, "What has God done?" and then formulates a response to the world based upon God's gracious love rather than emotions or logic.

Scripture tells us that (Rm 14:23) *"everything that does not come from faith is sin."* When people hear this passage from Romans for the first time it often makes many people feel depressed. When we consider the number of times we act without reference to our faith it quickly becomes apparent that we are sinning constantly. Fear not, however, for Christ has already paid for these sins.

Until the day of death our old self will be our constant companion. Until death the voices of fear, guilt, worry, and doubt will constantly be whispering in our ear. Our brains will constantly be at work finding logical and rational reasons why we should succumb to these emotions, but if we turn to Christ and continue in his words of promise, he will set us free from the voices that would enslave us.

> (Rm 8:1-2) *"Therefore, there is now no condemnation for those who are in Christ Jesus, because through Christ Jesus the law of the Spirit of life set me free from the law of sin and death."*

Emotional reasoning is conquered by recognizing every fear, every doubt, and every worry, as a sign that we have forgotten some gracious promise that God has made. Recognizing this, the Christian then focuses on God's grace and mercy, and searches for a positive promise from God to address and overcome these negative emotions. Our response to life is led by grace, rather than driven by emotion.

Lesson 9 ~ Weekly Activities

Reviewing Cognitive Distortions

Continue to examine your thinking styles so that you can better recognize distorted, negative thinking, and replace it with gospel centered positive thinking. Use the Law ~ Gospel Thinking Cards and the tools in the **Appendix** to help you identify these distortions and replace them with gospel centered alternatives. Make sure to analyze, in written form, at least one distortion every day.

Caring for the Body and Spirit God Gave me

Remember that you are body, mind, and spirit and do not neglect your body as we focus on mind and spirit issues. Continue to track your sleep, diet, and exercise routines. Discuss your progress with your support partner. Talk about your other life style changes such as spending more time talking, playing music, or adding other activities to your day.

Scripture Reading

For your daily Scripture reading you are encouraged to read the entire Gospel of John (about three chapters a day). The guided readings below, which should be mixed in throughout the week, address the relationship of emotions to our decision making, and the role that faith can play in our emotional reactions to situations.

Day 2 ~ Read John 18:28 - 19:16

Did Pilate think Jesus deserved to die?

Did Pilate want to free Jesus and believe that freeing Jesus was the "right" thing to do?

What emotion kept Pilate from doing what he knew in his heart was right and good?

Day 4 ~ Read Mark 14:60-72 and Acts 5:17-33

What emotion made Peter deny Jesus?

How are Peter's actions before the resurrection different from his actions after the resurrection?

What changed in Peter's life to make him act so differently?

Day 6 ~ Read Luke 8:40-56 and John 11:1-53

In both of these Bible accounts Jesus was told about someone who was gravely ill. Instead of going right away, Jesus waited. If it was your brother or daughter who was dying, how would Jesus' delay make you feel?

How would you feel about Jesus after being told your daughter or brother had died (while he waited)?

What kind of attitude did Jairus and Martha display toward Jesus after their loved ones died and why?

- NOTES -

- NOTES -

Lesson 10
The Distortions of "Should Statements" and "Labeling"

What's the Point? *Focusing on what life "should" be like we often fail to see God's blessing in what life already is. This lesson confronts the distortion of "should statements" by finding God's grace in places where our sinful nature would never seek him. The distortion of "labeling" is overcome by replacing our vision of ourselves and others with God's vision of us through Christ.*

What Can We Expect from Life?

In this form of thinking people dwell on the way they should be, or others should be. When this preoccupation with "shoulds" is directed against ourselves, the result is frustration and guilt. When this preoccupation is directed against others, the result is frustration and anger. To review:

8. SHOULD STATEMENTS

You try to motivate yourself with "should" and "shouldn't," as if you had to be whipped and punished before you could be expected to do anything. "Musts" and "oughts" are also offenders. When you address "should" statements at yourself the emotional consequences are guilt. When you direct "should" statements toward others, you feel anger, frustration, and resentment.

Examples

a. *You are angry at work all day because your boss did not recognize the extra effort you made to finish a project! ("should" directed at others)*

b. *You feel guilty every time you look at your child because of a scar they bear from an accident. You say to yourself, "I should have never let them go out and play!" (directed at self)*

c. *You were busy doing a million things other people had asked you to do. Somebody becomes angry at you for the one thing you didn't get done after an exhausting day. You feel both guilty and frustrated. You say to yourself, "I know I should have done that first!" (directed at self and others)*

"Should," "ought," and "must" statements suggest a desire to change reality when the only real choice is between accepting or not accepting it. For example, "The boss should show greater appreciation for the hard work I do!" The mental preoccupation of the employee becomes what the boss doesn't do and likely will never do. Anger and frustration build the longer the employee contemplates this reality.

When directed toward oneself the statement might be, "I should be making a million dollars a year by now!" Circumstances may be such that the person has never had an opportunity to achieve such a specific job or income goal. As the person dwells on this fact they become frustrated or feel guilty, falsely attributing their circumstance to their own inadequacies.

Not all "should" statements contain the word "should." For example "Why can't I get ahead in this world?" Or, "If only I had stayed with my last job?" Behind all the "should have," "could have," and "if only" thoughts lay the fundamental belief that different circumstances would make life better. This is the proverbial "The grass is always greener on the other side" style of thinking.

In secular cognitive therapy individuals stuck in this kind of thinking style are encouraged to focus on accepting the present reality, rather than brooding over some possible reality. The "Serenity Prayer," attributed to Reinhold Neibuhr (1926), provides a convenient model for this type of therapeutic approach.

God grant us the serenity

to accept the things we cannot change,

courage to change the things we can,

and wisdom to know the difference.

While this prayer seeking the aid of God adorns many a Christian home, a closer look at the prayer reveals that it is not based in any hope. It speaks of accepting things we can't change, but it fails to supply any fundamental reasons for doing so.

A truly Christian approach to "should" thinking moves beyond the mere acceptance of reality to the discovery of hope within every reality.

The ultimate reality revealed in the gospel is that even in the things that we cannot change, God is there. One particular account of Scripture serves to illustrate this point.

After Jacob tricked his father Isaac into blessing him, he had to flee for his life because Esau his brother had sworn to kill him. As he flees toward the land of his Uncle Laban, Jacob stops to rest in some nameless place. Jacob is by himself, on the run, with no one to offer any comfort. During that night God reveals himself to him. Angels appear on a stairway reaching to heaven, ascending and descending.

It is interesting that, in Christian music, this event has been switched from a moment of God descending to man, to a moment of man trying to ascend to God. A traditional children's song, rooted in an African American spiritual, begins "I am climbing Jacob's ladder." The scriptural account of this event has nothing to do with man climbing, but with God descending from his throne to aid man. It is here, in this lonely deserted place, that Jacob receives promises from God.

Study and Discuss

Read Genesis 28:12-17

v. 15 What promises does Jacob receive from God?

v. 16 What does Jacob learn about God's presence?

Read Matthew 28:18-20 and Hebrews 13:5

What promise have we received from Christ?

Read Psalm 139:1-10

Is there a place where God's hand cannot reach?

Whenever "should" thinking enters the Christian's mind we need to return to the wonderful promise of Scripture that wherever we are in life,

God is there. It doesn't matter if life turns one direction or another, or if people around us change in this way or that. Psalm 139 reminds us, *"If I rise on the wings of the dawn, if I settle on the far side of the sea, even there your hand will guide me, your right hand will hold me fast."*

There is not a place we can be where God cannot touch us with his grace and blessing. The grass is not greener on the other side, but to borrow from Psalm 23, wherever the Good Shepherd makes us lie down, there we will find "green pastures." A gospel centered therapy does not merely focus on an acceptance of the present reality. Rather, it focuses on God's promise that the place where we are is a place of his presence and blessing. One of the great biblical examples of a life based on this hopeful model is the life of Joseph.

Joseph was the favored son of Jacob through his wife Rachel. His favored status was not appreciated by his half brothers. At the age of seventeen, God revealed to Joseph through dreams that he would rule over his brothers and also his father (Gn 37). The Scripture does not record that God told Joseph to communicate this to his brothers, and no doubt a little sinful pride was at the root of Joseph's announcement of these dreams.

An opportunity arises for the brothers to pay back Joseph's arrogance, and so Joseph is sold to slave traders. To a seventeen-year-old spoiled rich kid this is a major tragedy. To this tragedy, however, Joseph responds by being the best slave he can be (Gn 39). Joseph earns the respect of his master, Potiphar, and eventually rises in status to become Potiphar's personal attendant. Potiphar turns all of his household affairs over to Joseph.

Joseph's new life was not what it "should" have been, but it wasn't a bad life. However, the bad news in Joseph's life was not over. Potiphar's wife lusts after Joseph, and though Joseph is able to resist temptation, he is falsely accused of adultery and throne into jail by Potiphar (Gn 39:20).

Ancient jails did not have hot showers, cable T.V., or three square meals a day. What hope did Joseph have of release when the captain of Pharoah's guard believed he had committed adultery? There would be no DNA testing to prove his innocence, and no supreme court to which he could appeal his case. Joseph, however, responds to this tragedy as he did the first, by becoming the best prisoner he can be.

Joseph becomes so trusted by the warden that he winds up running the prison.

> (Gn 39:22-23) *"So the warden put Joseph in charge of all those held in the prison, and he was made responsible for all that was done there. The warden paid no attention to anything under Joseph's care, because the LORD was with Joseph and gave him success in whatever he did."*

Tragedy again would strike Joseph. A slim hope of a reprieve presents itself when he interprets some dreams of the Pharaoh's cupbearer and baker. The price for these interpretations is that (Gn 40:14) *"when all goes well with you, remember me and show me kindness; mention me to Pharaoh and get me out of this prison."*

All does go well for the cupbearer, but when he leaves prison, he does not mention Joseph to Pharaoh for a period of two years. At this point, despair on Joseph's part would be so easy to understand. He had tasted wealth and everything good that life of that period had to offer. Now, all he could look forward to was life in prison. Joseph's best chance for a reprieve was gone. Who would blame him for being angry and frustrated with himself and others?

The life of Joseph does eventually change. He is finally remembered by the cupbearer when the Pharaoh experiences some troubling dreams. While the life experience of Joseph dramatically changes, his approach to those experiences does not. As a slave he was the best slave he could be, and as a prisoner he was the best prisoner he could be. Now as Pharaoh's servant, Joseph continues to serve as best he can, and rises to *"second in command"* (Gn 41:43) in Egypt.

During a famine that follows, Joseph's brothers come to Egypt to buy bread. The family is brought back together and comes to live in Egypt under Joseph's care. When Jacob finally dies, the brothers are concerned that Joseph will take revenge, and at that point Joseph reveals the theology that had guided him throughout his tragedies.

> (Gen 50:18-21) *"His brothers then came and threw themselves down before him. 'We are your slaves,' they said. But Joseph said to them, 'Don't be afraid. Am I in the place of God? You intended to harm me, but God intended it for good to accomplish what is now being done, the saving of many lives. So then, don't*

be afraid. I will provide for you and your children.' And he reassured them and spoke kindly to them."

Joseph understood that God was present with his blessing even in the tragedies he experienced in life. His words are virtually echoed in the verse from Paul in Romans, (Rm 8:28) *"And we know that in all things God works for the good of those who love him, who have been called according to his purpose."*

Throughout his life Joseph could have been swallowed up by despair and frustration with others. Instead of focusing on what others should have done, or what he could have done differently, he focused on what he could do now. His words to his brothers reveal that this attitude was not rooted in a simple acceptance of reality, but a belief that God was there and had a blessed purpose for whatever confronted him.

When "should" thinking begins to take over in our lives, Christians need to wake up from their dream world and confess with Jacob (Gn 28:16), *"Surely the LORD is in this place, and I was not aware of it."* We need to recall the words of the Psalmist (Ps 139:9-10), *"If I rise on the wings of the dawn, if I settle on the far side of the sea, even there your hand will guide me, your right hand will hold me fast."* Life lived in Christ is life as it should be wherever, whenever, and however it is lived. The pastures aren't greener on the other side, but our good shepherd (Ps 23:2), *"makes us lie down in green pastures.*"

WHO ARE WE?

We are both "saint" and "sinner." No matter how long you may have been a Christian, Satan still continues to live inside of you telling you that you are unworthy of love because of your sin. He tells you that you are a failure for the many times you have not lived up to your potential as measured by yourself, others, and God. Yet, in Christ, this is not the only portrait of ourselves.

In Christ we are perfect. In him you (1Co 6:11) *"were washed, you were sanctified, you were justified in the name of the Lord Jesus Christ and by the Spirit of our God."* Within Scripture the labels of saint or sinner can both be applicable to the Christian and neither label is to be rejected. Secular cognitive therapy, however, views all negative labeling as a destructive form of thinking defined in the following manner:

9. LABELING AND MISLABELING

This is an extreme form of over-generalization. Instead of describing your error, you attach a negative label to yourself. "I'm a loser." When someone else's behavior rubs you the wrong way, you attach a negative label to him: "He's a louse!" Mislabeling involves describing an event with language that is highly colored and emotionally loaded.

a. *Your spouse comes home and asks if dinner will be ready soon. You haven't started anything because you were busy with other family obligations (transporting children, helping with projects, cleaning). You mumble aloud, "No, its not. I'm just a lousy... (wife/husband)!"*

b. *Your child has not cleaned their room in the last week. You enter the bedroom, look around, and say, "You are such a slob!"*

c. *Someone tries to explain some (homework, work skill, etc.) to you and you do not understand the concept well after the first explanation. You exclaim, "I'm so stupid!"*

Secular cognitive therapy views negative labeling as destructive because it attacks the very identity of a person. At the heart of this secular approach is actually a theological viewpoint that says, *"just because you do bad things, that doesn't make you a bad person!"* Negative labels are viewed in this theological point of view as damaging to our self-esteem. However, deep inside the human spirit, the refusal to equate our deeds with our being often rings hollow. "If I'm not a stupid person, then why did I just do such a stupid thing?" "If my entire family is upset with the way I'm living my life, then why am I not a lousy person?"

As mentioned in Lesson 5, even Sigmund Freud once said that if a patient: *"represents his ego to us as worthless, incapable of any achievement and morally despicable . . . He must surely be right in some way"*[68] Scripture itself teaches:

---

[68]Freud, Sigmund, "Collected Papers", 1917 (Translated by Joan Riviere, Vol. IV, chapter 8, "Mourning and Melancholia", pp. 155-156. London: Hogarth Press Ltd., 1952

(Lk 6:43-45) *"No good tree bears bad fruit, nor does a bad tree bear good fruit. . . . The good man brings good things out of the good stored up in his heart, and the evil man brings evil things out of the evil stored up in his heart. For out of the overflow of his heart his mouth speaks."*

While the labels we apply to ourselves or others can, at times, be inaccurate and based on faulty information, the labels that often hurt the most are the ones that have some basis in objective reality. Just as a good joke often plays on a kernel of truth, so also the labels we apply to ourselves and others often reflect an inner truth.

People don't just commit sins, the plain Biblical truth is that we are "sinners." David writes, (Ps 51:5) *"Surely I was sinful at birth, sinful from the time my mother conceived me."* The Christian approach to this thinking style is not the rejection of labeling outright, but a right understanding of the truth that labels sometimes reveal and an effective means of dealing with the painful truth that labels highlight.

Fundamentally the Christian approach to labeling is rooted in a right understanding of the use of "law and gospel." As discussed earlier, the gospel is the good news we have in Christ, particularly the good news of forgiveness and eternal life we have in him.

The goal of the gospel is to encourage us and offer hope to the repentant sinner. The gospel offers us a foundation for living the life God designed for us. The goal of the law, on the other hand, is to crush the unrepentant sinner. The law of God includes his commands, along with the threats and punishments for breaking those commands.

The goal of the law is to lead us to despair of our sinful ways and our own methods of dealing with sin. Our only option from this state of despair is to turn to God's grace for hope and deliverance. The function of the law is primarily diagnostic. The law leads us to call out to God for help, but our help is only provided in the gospel. In carrying out this function the law can be brutal in its labeling. Take for instance the words of Jesus against the Pharisees:

(Mt 23:28-33) *"on the outside you appear to people as righteous but on the inside you are full of hypocrisy and wickedness. Woe to you, teachers of the law and Pharisees, . . . You snakes! You brood of vipers! How will you escape being condemned to hell?"*

Obviously Jesus was not afraid to use labels. The law can be brutal in its condemnation, but the gospel provides a comfort that erases the pain. The Psalmist offers an example of the sweet words that God offers to the condemned sinner. The Psalmist says that God:

> (Ps 103:9-13) *"will not always accuse, nor will he harbor his anger forever; he does not treat us as our sins deserve or repay us according to our iniquities. For as high as the heavens are above the earth, so great is his love for those who fear him; as far as the east is from the west, so far has he removed our transgressions from us. As a father has compassion on his children, so the LORD has compassion on those who fear him."*

In dealing with ourselves and others the fundamental issue is not whether a particular label is accurate, but whether or not it is the appropriate word someone needs to hear. One of the ways that the Bible shows itself to be divinely revealed is the consistency with which it applies the two messages of "Law and Gospel."

Within Scripture the law of God is consistently applied to the unrepentant; that is, the person who does not want to change how they think about sin. The gospel is always applied to the repentant, who wants to change their life, no matter what sins they have committed. The Old and New Testaments always follow this pattern of applying the law and the gospel. The parable of the pharisee and the tax collector offers an excellent example of the proper use of law and gospel.

Study and Discuss

Read Luke 18:9-14

Why does Jesus tell this parable (see v. 9)?

Who is denied forgiveness and how did he label himself?

Who receives forgiveness and how did he label himself?

The bottom line is that in life we don't just sometimes do stupid things. The truth is, we can be stupid people. We don't simply commit failures. We often are failures. We don't just commit sins. We are sinners. The Christian, however, does not fear these labels. While they may accurately define the sinner in us, they do not define who we are in Christ.

The Christian lives in the paradox of being two people at once. The Christian is at one in the same time a saint and a sinner. When we begin to listen to and follow the sinner living inside of us (our old Adam), words of law need to unmask our evil nature. The law must lead us to be thoroughly disgusted with our sinful self so that we turn from our sin and turn to God and his grace for help. When we stop listening to that old Adam and turn to God for his grace he now addresses us as a new person, perfect and holy, without any stain, spot or blemish.

As much as we would like to be seen only as perfect people, the truth is that until we put off our sinful nature in death we will always be both a saint and sinner. What label fits us at any given moment? For the Christian this question is not answered by simply denying the validity of a label (I'm not a bad person, I just do bad things!), or in simply accepting a label (I am a bad person because I have done bad things).

God determines the label that best describes us based upon our attitude toward our sin and God's grace to us in Christ. Who we are is no longer determined by our sin, for we all (Rm 3:23-24) *"have sinned and fall short of the glory of God, and are justified freely by his grace through the redemption that came by Christ Jesus."* God now labels us based on whether we are repentant or unrepentant.

When we try to stand or fall before God based upon our own works, the label we will receive is "condemned sinner." If we confess our sins, and stand before God on the basis of his grace, the label we will receive is "perfect child," for the sake of Christ. In dealing with others, Christians should be guided by these same principles.

Christ himself was both vicious in condemnation, and compassionate in forgiveness. The words of Christ were not governed by the sins that had been committed by people, but by their attitude toward their sin. (Luke 1:53) *"He has filled the hungry with good things but has sent the rich away empty."* (Luke 5:31-32) *"It is not the healthy who need a doctor, but the sick. I have not come to call the righteous, but sinners to repentance."*

The consistent word of God applied to those who don't think they need forgiveness and grace through scripture is law. The consistent word of God applied to those who despise their sin and feel powerless to overcome it is forgiveness. (1 John 1:8-9) *"If we claim to be without sin, we deceive ourselves and the truth is not in us. If we confess our sins, he is faithful and just and will forgive us our sins and purify us from all unrighteousness."*

Lesson 10 ~ Weekly Activities

Reviewing Cognitive Distortions

Continue to examine your thinking styles so that you can better recognize distorted, negative thinking, and replace it with gospel centered positive thinking. Use the Law ~ Gospel Thinking Cards to help you identify these distortions and resolve these distortions with gospel centered thinking. Write down at least one distortion per day using the tools in the **Appendix**.

Caring for the Body and Spirit God Gave me

Remember that you are body, mind, and spirit and do not neglect your body as we focus on mind and spirit issues. Continue to track your sleep, diet, and exercise routines using the tools in the appendix. Discuss your progress with your support partner. Talk about your other life style changes such as spending more time talking, playing music, or adding other activities to your day.

Scripture Reading

For your daily Scripture reading you are encouraged to read the entire book of Genesis. As you read Genesis consider how many times people, beginning with Adam and Eve, destroyed their lives by believing that they could have a better life than the one God already gave them. In addition to this daily reading, mix in the following readings throughout the week and answer the following questions.

Day 2 ~ Read Psalm 103

Does God treat us the way we "should" be treated (v. 10)?

Why does God have compassion on us (v. 13-17)?

Day 4 ~ Read Romans 5:1-11

What type of negative labels could God apply to us?

How did God deal with all the negatives he saw in us?

Day 6 ~ Psalm 130 and 1 Corinthians 13

Does God keep a record of sins?

Why not?

Instead of focusing on the sins of others, what does love focus on?

- NOTES -

Lesson 11
The Distortion of "Personalization"

What's the Point? *At times we think that everybody is out to get us, or that everything we've done, or will do, will have a negative outcome. Everything revolves around us! The cognitive distortion of "personalization" is overcome by trusting in God's promise that he will deliver us from every evil. Even if the world is against us, God fights for us, and he will let nothing separate us from his love.*

Who Is in Control of the World?

In this final form of thinking, people assume that the words or actions of others are always some kind of reaction to themselves. This form of thinking may also be labeled paranoia. If you see an angry friend, you immediately assume the friend is angry at you. Seeing a group of friends gathered together laughing you presume the group is making fun of you. Someone you see whispering must be spreading gossip about you. Everyone at work is out to get you, everyone in your family wishes you would just go away. To review:

10. PERSONALIZATION

You see yourself as the cause of some negative external event, which in fact you were not primarily responsible for.

a. *When you were a young child, your parents got divorced and you thought you must have done something wrong that made this happen.*

b. *Your child is doing poorly in school. You blame yourself for not spending enough time with the child.*

c. *Someone dies from a heart attack. You blame yourself for their death because you did not react quickly enough, you were out shopping and should have been home, you didn't perform CPR properly, or didn't encourage that person to go to a doctor when they had mentioned they weren't feeling well.*

Small children may use this form of thinking as they try to interpret events in their family life. Divorce is often personalized by children and they think they had something to do with it. Sometimes when a family tragedy or illness closely follows in time a child's misbehavior, they interpret the event as their fault. Thus, those using "personalization" as a style of thinking not only see the behaviors of others revolving around themselves, but even uncontrollable events, illnesses, accidents, and the like. Within this style of thinking there is an overwhelming sense of being out of control, since so many forces are aligned against you.

Many of the Psalms seem to reflect this style of thinking. However, in David's case, he wasn't being paranoid. David's complaints reflected reality. Sometimes when you think everybody is out to get you, they really are! Many of David's Psalms resonate with those trapped in this mode of thinking.

Study and Discuss

Read Psalm 41:4-9 and 69:1-4

How did David see the world around him?

While it may be true in some isolated situations that the whole world is out to get you, in most situations this style of thinking is extremely egocentric, bordering on the grandiose. It is the back side of arrogance and pride, where we give far more negative weight to our individual actions than they merit. We see ourselves as the negative center of attention for everything and everybody around us.

While personalization is a back handed type of arrogance, it leaves a person feeling completely powerless against sin and its effects. Either the individual feels powerless because of the sins others are committing, or the individual feels powerless to control the effects that their own sins have upon others.

In secular cognitive therapy the individual will be taught to minimize the role they envision for their life. If someone else is angry, they will be taught to think first, "They are angry about something, but they are not necessarily angry at me." They will be encouraged to envision their lives as having less direct impact on the lives of others. Accidents happen! Other people are ultimately responsible for their own actions.

While these are important corrective actions to take in our thinking process, they still do not address the core issue behind this thinking; namely, our own inability to overcome the power of sin in our lives. When in those rare circumstances, like King David's, where "the whole world is out to get me!" these corrective thinking actions are powerless to improve our mental outlook. The answer for King David in his moments of despair was not a more rational form of thinking, but the hope provided by faith!

Study and Discuss

Read Psalm 41:10-13 and Psalm 69:6, 33-36

What certainty does David cling to in the midst of his despair?

David does not rest his hope in his ability to overcome his own shortcomings, or the attacks of his enemies. His hope rests in God's ability to save us. God saves us from our own sin, and he rescues us from the sins of others.

Ultimately God's saving work is rooted in the cross of Jesus Christ, but too often we relegate God's saving work to life after death, and not the life we live now. The power to stop focusing on what others can do to us lies in the realization that right now, (Ps 46:7) *"The LORD Almighty is with us; the God of Jacob is our fortress."*

Study and Discuss

Read Psalm 56:3-4 and Psalm 118:5-6

Why is David unafraid of what others can do to him?

Read Romans 8:31-39

Who can separate us from God's love?

How does God rescue us now? God's power to save can come in many forms. We have the resources of family, friends, co-workers, and particularly the church to call upon. Sometimes God rescues us from the forces aligned against us not by an ability or strength we have, but through the resources he has given others. As the apostle Paul points out, each of us has different gifts.

> *"Just as each of us has one body with many members, and these members do not all have the same function, so in Christ we who are many form one body, and each member belongs to all the others. We have different gifts, according to the grace given us."* (Rm 12:4-6)

It's easy to think you are all alone in the world and no one will help you if you never ask anyone for help from fear or pride. Part of living under grace is allowing God to help you through other people. Why should God do some miracle when he has already provided the answer to your prayer in a person you see every day, or every week.

God rescues us in other ways. Sometimes he simply gives us the strength, patience, or abilities we need to endure troubles. Frequently our imaginations amplify the consequences of the troubles we face beyond reality. We feel totally abandoned and alone, when God has already given us what we need to conquer a particular challenge. Millions of people have uttered the phrase, "I don't know how I'm going to get through this" facing a challenge in life, and on the other side of the challenge said, "That wasn't so bad after all."

Our fears often grow from an ignorance of what God has already given us, but has not called upon us to use. Resources already around us, or our own individual gifts and talents, may have fully equipped us to meet some challenge, but because we have never had to use these resources, gifts, or talents, we can only rely on faith in God and his promise to care for us to calm our fears.

In addition to providing normal resources, God can also do miracles to help us in our time of need. However, in waiting for miracles, Christians must always remember that the greatest miracle of all is something God has already guaranteed to us in Christ. That miracle, is the gift of the resurrection which God bestows upon all who trust in Christ. It is ultimately trust in this miracle that inspired Martin Luther to write the closing words to the hymn, "A Mighty Fortress", based on Psalm 46.

"And take they our life, Goods, fame, child and wife,
Let these all be gone, they yet have nothing won;
the Kingdom ours remaineth."

As a pastor visiting my members in the hospital, I like to gently remind them that this is the greatest miracle by occasionally offering them a choice of prayers. Occasionally I will tell my members, based on the example of the apostle Paul, who said, (Php 1:23) *"I desire to depart and be with Christ, which is better by far,"* that I can pray for the worst case scenario, or the best case scenario.

The best case scenario would be that God would permanently heal them of their troubles by taking them out of this sinful and painful world to the glorious life we are promised in heaven. The worst case scenario would be that the doctors are highly successful, that the mortal body is restored, and that they must go on living in this sinful and troubled world. I then conclude by asking my members if they want me to pray for the worst case scenario, or the best case scenario. Amazingly, they all ask me to pray for the worst case scenario!

There is nothing, including death itself, from which God cannot rescue us. Not only does God rescue us from what others can do to us, but he also rescues others from what we might do to them.

Personalization includes an excessive fear of the negative ways our life has, or will, impact the lives of others. This fear has a paralyzing effect. Indecision and inaction are the hallmarks of a life governed by this type of fear, even when reason and logic cry out for a decisive action. When decisions are put off, or action stalled, more trouble in life follows.

Christians need not have this fear, for the same God who shields us also loves the whole world. All the promises we have reviewed throughout these lessons not only apply to us, but to everyone touched by our lives. God not only protects you from others, he also protects others from you.

Study and Discuss

Read John 10:27-29

What promise does Jesus give with regard to all of his sheep?

Read Ezekiel 18:20-23

If someone perishes, whose fault is it?

Ultimately Christ is in control of this world. He says, (Mt 28:18) *"All authority in heaven and on earth has been given to me."* This does not mean that we are powerless to make choices in life (including bad choices), but it does mean that (Rm 8:39) *"neither height nor depth, nor anything else in all creation, will be able to separate us from the love of God that is in Christ Jesus our Lord."*

God delivers us from the many ways that others harm us, but he is also at work delivering others from the ways we may harm them. Faith in this all encompassing love gives us the power to act when others would be paralyzed with fear. The book of Esther provides a wonderful example of this type of faith at work.

The book of Esther is somewhat unique in Scripture in that God is never mentioned by name. However, faith in God and his mercy toward Israel is a thread woven into the very fabric of this book.

Esther was a Jew who had become a favored wife to King Xerxes; however, her nationality was not known to the King. Because her uncle Mordecai would not bow down, for religious reasons, to a high official named Haman, Haman convinced King Xerxes to have all Jews throughout the kingdom annihilated. If Esther's nationality was revealed, she herself might be killed. Nevertheless, Mordecai approaches her and makes a request for her help.

Study and Discuss

Read Esther 4:6-16

According to verse 14, what does Mordecai believe will happen to the Jews if Esther fails to act?

What does Mordecai believe is the reason Esther became a queen?

Is Esther worried that she might be killed and fail?

Imagine the sense of personal guilt Mordecai could have felt knowing that the total annihilation of the Jewish race might be the result of his stubborn refusal to cling to a Jewish custom and not bow down. Imagine the anxiety that Esther could have felt knowing that the total annihilation of her people and her own life may hinge on what she did next. However, after reading the scriptural text, one gains a sense that these people are neither overwhelmed by guilt nor overcome with anxiety. Their relative peace facing tremendous challenges is the result of their belief that God will act on behalf of his people. No matter what others may threaten, no matter what they might have done, no matter what they might do, God will take care of his people.

God's grace extends to all people. No sin of ours is so great that it can snatch someone from God's hands. No sin that someone else may commit is so great that it can destroy us. People may perish eternally. We might even be a tool that Satan uses to bring this about, but the ultimate responsibility for personal salvation lies with the individual.

God can save anyone even if we (Es 4:14) *"remain silent at this time."* Even when we fail to help someone God wanted us to help, *"relief and deliverance . . . will arise from another place."*

God tells us these things not to give us an excuse to sin. Anyone who has ever experienced the joy of being God's agent for bringing someone to Christ wouldn't want to forsake an opportunity to be a witness. However, Christ himself was concerned that the fear of making mistakes might cripple people in their personal witness. Thus, he tells his own disciples.

> (Mt 10:19-20) *"But when they arrest you, do not worry about what to say or how to say it. At that time you will be given what to say, for it will not be you speaking, but the Spirit of your Father speaking through you."*

While life may be difficult at times, there is never reason for despair. God does not call upon us to meet a challenge, without also providing us with those resources we need to conquer all that life throws at us.

Study and Discuss

Read 1 Corinthians 10:13

What promise does God make to us in this verse?

Why might belief in the first part of this verse be essential to believing in the promise?

Personalization can include an attitude which views our problems as unique to ourselves. "Nobody understands me!" "Nobody knows what I am going through!" This type of thinking excludes others from helping us, and ignores a fundamental aspect of God's relationship to us.

Study and Discuss

Read Hebrews 2:14 - 3:1 and Hebrews 4:14-16

Why did God's Son take on human flesh?

There is nothing you can experience that God himself hasn't experienced through Christ. God thoroughly understands our weaknesses and frailty. God became man so that we would trust him more completely. The almighty God took on weak human flesh in the person of Christ, and through that flesh accomplished our eternal salvation. Through Christ we learn that the weaknesses of others does not prevent God from using them as tools to bring blessings to us.

Study and Discuss

Read 2 Corinthians 4:5-7

Through what vehicle does God reveal his glory?

Paul spoke the words of 2 Corinthians out of amazement that God would choose himself to be the vehicle of proclaiming Christ in this world. Paul knew that when God chose him to be an apostle, God could not have found a more ugly jar of clay.

Paul had been a persecutor of the church and a murderer of Christians. It was a constant source of wonder to the apostle Paul that God specifically called him on the road to Damascus to be his chief witness to the Gentile world. Why would God do such a thing? Why wouldn't God choose something more perfect, like the angels, to be his witnesses in this world? Paul explains this mystery in his letter to Timothy.

Study and Discuss

Read 1 Timothy 1:15-16

Why did God choose Paul as his witness?

As we grow in our knowledge of God's grace, we learn that God can use weaknesses, failures and even death itself to bring blessings to his people. As we grow in this understanding, our fear of what others can do to us, or what we can do to others, is diminished.

The distortion of "Personalization" is rooted in the fear of what others can do to us, or the evil our actions can inflict upon others. Through faith in God's grace, we learn that this fear is baseless.

> (Ps 118:6-7) *"The LORD is with me; I will not be afraid. What can man do to me? The LORD is with me; he is my helper. I will look in triumph on my enemies."*

As we have noted before (see "over-generalization" or "negative prediction"), this belief that we can triumph in all circumstances is intimately linked to a right understanding of what is good. "Good," as defined by Scripture, revolves around Christ, the saving of souls, and the building up of his eternal kingdom.

Apart from a life focused on the good that God wants to accomplish, it is often impossible to find good in what happens in our life. When our lives are focused upon God and good as he would define it, everything in life changes. The innocent death of God's beloved Son, falsely accused, deserted by his friends, nailed to a cross, becomes the means through which God saves the world. While the whole world, at one point, seemed aligned against Christ, this event is the greatest positive of all time. In a similar way, our response to persecution, insult, etc., is a tool through which God may bring blessings to others.

Study and Discuss

Read Titus 2:9-10 and 1 Peter 2:18-21

Why should slaves be submissive to harsh masters?

Read 1 Peter 3:1-3

Why should wives be submissive to husbands who are not believers?

The distortion of "Personalization" is ultimately rooted in the fear that we are at the mercy of others. Once we realize that we are in the mercy of an almighty God who loves us, we gain the power to control our fears and live a life rooted in love for others, rather than in fear of what others might do to us, or fear of what we can do to others.

- NOTES -

Lessons Summary

While the principles of secular psychology are often at odds with the preaching of the gospel, some of their tools and insights can be useful to Christians as we seek to apply the gospel to the human heart. As a beginning point for this assistance, modern research into depression clearly contradicts the prevailing myth in the American culture that depression is primarily a medical condition. While chemical imbalances may exist in the brain, and these imbalances may be partially corrected by medication, the medications do not fundamentally alter the forces that are usually responsible for driving us into severe and chronic depression.

The high relapse rate of individuals treated only with medication, versus the low relapse rate of people who receive medication and therapy, provides ample evidence that the fundamentals of depression lie in how we interpret our world. While medications treat the emotional symptoms of depression, they do not address the underlying cause. Even the federal government recognizes this fact. In its own publications which advise our nation on depression treatment it states:

> *Most do best with combined treatment: medication to gain relatively quick symptom relief and psychotherapy to learn more effective ways to deal with life's problems, including depression.*[69]

The gospel is the way that God wants us to deal with life's problems, but even Christians who know the gospel, fail to employ it in dealing with life. Depression cannot be dealt with as a purely medical issue, but must be seen in the wider context of our relationship to God and our understanding of his grace. Even when addressing the physical matters that can contribute to depression (poor sleep patterns, poor diet, etc.) the Christian recognizes that there is an intimate link between a stressed life style and a failure to incorporate spiritual principles into our life.

Unfortunately, a specific ministry to people suffering from clinical depression is virtually nonexistent in Christian congregations. Contrary even to federal government guidelines, most people seek relief from their depression and anxiety solely in medications. We treat the symptoms, while the underlying causes grow unchecked.

---

[69] "Depression" (NIH Publication No. 02-3561 Printed 2000, Reprinted Sept. 2002)

The fundamental path to peace and joy laid out in Scripture begins with repentance. To live a repentant life is, scripturally speaking, to change the way we think. What needs to change in our thinking? We need to make the gospel of Jesus Christ, the "good news," the focal point of how we think!

(Mk 1:14-15) *"After John was put in prison, Jesus went into Galilee, proclaiming the good news of God. 'The time has come,' he said. 'The kingdom of God is near. Repent and believe the good news!'"*

The gospel of Jesus Christ provides a unique way of changing our thinking that can lift us out of depression and into a positive outlook on life. The cognitive distortions identified by secular psychologists provide the Christian with a helpful model for identifying deficiencies in how we think. They are tools of the law which tell us in specific ways what is wrong with our thinking.

The deficiency of secular psychology lies in identifying how our thinking must change. Secular psychology is unable to talk about hope that lies beyond a logical evaluation of our life. Interestingly enough, secular cognitive therapists have, however, recognized the powerful role that hope has in treating depression. Within the last several years they have even developed inventories to measure how hopeful people are.

One recent study among the elderly showed that people who scored high on an inventory designed to measure hopeful feelings were far less likely to be depressed than people who saw little to be hopeful about.[70] While secular psychology can, to a limited degree measure hope, it cannot offer to its patients the type of hope God offers to us in the gospel. Will we be completely forgiven? What will happen to us when we die? Will we ever know real and unconditional love? Secular psychology cannot offer certainties regarding these questions. The gospel does!

Without the gospel as a tool to resolve certain thinking styles, secular cognitive therapists sometimes distort the truth that God has revealed in Scripture in order to devise an alternative solution. For

---

[70]Chimich, William T., MD, FRCPC1; Nekolaichuk, Cheryl L ., PhD2; "Exploring the Links Between Depression, Integrity, and Hope in the Elderly" (Canadian Journal of Psychiatry 2004;49:428–433)

instance, to resolve "all or nothing" thinking, secular therapists are forced to replace God's black and white standards with shades of gray.

What shade of gray will we measure ourselves by? Secular therapists tell us that the choice is ours. There are no real absolutes. Truth is relative. We become our own gods and set our own standards. While this attitude may be supported by popular culture, there is an inner voice of the law that God has left inside each one of us. This voice still condemns us no matter what personal standards we choose to live by, no matter what our culture says is right and wrong.

Ultimately, the depressing facts of life cannot be dealt with through any action or thought process that we sinful humans can devise. It is God's Holy Spirit working in our hearts through the gospel that alone has the power to defeat depression.

The thoughts that lead to depression are natural to us. The gospel is not natural to us. The thoughts that lead to depression are so automatic and deeply ingrained that while we live in this world we must constantly be renewed and refreshed in "gospel thinking." Medications can't do this, nor can secular psychologists. The only place to find renewal in the gospel is in God's word and sacraments, and among the people who share these things together; that is, the church.

It is my prayer that in the future the church will take a more active role in addressing mental illness, and that those who read this material may be renewed in their faith that in Christ we have the answers to all the questions of life. Those answers may include making use of the wonderful medical tools and therapies God has provided to us, but never to the exclusion of the specific help and aid that God gives us through his saving gospel in Jesus Christ.

- NOTES -

"Gospel Therapy"
A New Vision Of Life Through Christ

APPENDIX

Caring for the Body and Spirit God Gave Me

Sleep is continuous sleep, Naps less than 2 hours don't count.

Quality of Diet is rated 0-5 (0=very bad and 5 is very good)

Overall mood is rated 0-5 (0=bad day and 5 is great day)

Week 1 Beginning Date:

DAY	Hours Slept	Minutes of Exercise	Time in God's Word (Yes/No)	Rate Quality of Diet	Rate Overall Mood
1					
2					
3					
4					
5					
6					
7					

Week 2 Beginning Date:

DAY	Hours Slept	Minutes of Exercise	Time in God's Word (Yes/No)	Rate Quality of Diet	Rate Overall Mood
1					
2					
3					
4					
5					
6					
7					

Caring for the Body and Spirit God Gave me

Sleep is continuous sleep, Naps less than 2 hours don't count.

Quality of Diet is rated 0-5 (0=very bad and 5 is very good)

Overall mood is rated 0-5 (0=bad day and 5 is great day)

Week 3 Beginning Date:					
DAY	**Hours Slept**	**Minutes of Exercise**	**Time in God's Word (Yes/No)**	**Rate Quality of Diet**	**Rate Overall Mood**
1					
2					
3					
4					
5					
6					
7					

Week 4 Beginning Date:					
DAY	**Hours Slept**	**Minutes of Exercise**	**Time in God's Word (Yes/No)**	**Rate Quality of Diet**	**Rate Overall Mood**
1					
2					
3					
4					
5					
6					
7					

CARING FOR THE BODY AND SPIRIT GOD GAVE ME

Sleep is continuous sleep, Naps less than 2 hours don't count.

Quality of Diet is rated 0-5 (0=very bad and 5 is very good)

Overall mood is rated 0-5 (0=bad day and 5 is great day)

Week 5 Beginning Date:					
DAY	**Hours Slept**	**Minutes of Exercise**	**Time in God's Word (Yes/No)**	**Rate Quality of Diet**	**Rate Overall Mood**
1					
2					
3					
4					
5					
6					
7					

Week 6 Beginning Date:					
DAY	**Hours Slept**	**Minutes of Exercise**	**Time in God's Word (Yes/No)**	**Rate Quality of Diet**	**Rate Overall Mood**
1					
2					
3					
4					
5					
6					
7					

CARING FOR THE BODY AND SPIRIT GOD GAVE ME

Sleep is continuous sleep, Naps less than 2 hours don't count.

Quality of Diet is rated 0-5 (0=very bad and 5 is very good)

Overall mood is rated 0-5 (0=bad day and 5 is great day)

Week 7 Beginning Date:

DAY	Hours Slept	Minutes of Exercise	Time in God's Word (Yes/No)	Rate Quality of Diet	Rate Overall Mood
1					
2					
3					
4					
5					
6					
7					

Week 8 Beginning Date:

DAY	Hours Slept	Minutes of Exercise	Time in God's Word (Yes/No)	Rate Quality of Diet	Rate Overall Mood
1					
2					
3					
4					
5					
6					
7					

CARING FOR THE BODY AND SPIRIT GOD GAVE ME

Sleep is continuous sleep, Naps less than 2 hours don't count.
Quality of Diet is rated 0-5 (0=very bad and 5 is very good)
Overall mood is rated 0-5 (0=bad day and 5 is great day)

Week 9 Beginning Date:					
DAY	**Hours Slept**	**Minutes of Exercise**	**Time in God's Word (Yes/No)**	**Rate Quality of Diet**	**Rate Overall Mood**
1					
2					
3					
4					
5					
6					
7					

Week 10 Beginning Date:					
DAY	**Hours Slept**	**Minutes of Exercise**	**Time in God's Word (Yes/No)**	**Rate Quality of Diet**	**Rate Overall Mood**
1					
2					
3					
4					
5					
6					
7					

CARING FOR THE BODY AND SPIRIT GOD GAVE ME

Sleep is continuous sleep, Naps less than 2 hours don't count.

Quality of Diet is rated 0-5 (0=very bad and 5 is very good)

Overall mood is rated 0-5 (0=bad day and 5 is great day)

Week _____ Ongoing Beginning Date:					
DAY	**Hours Slept**	**Minutes of Exercise**	**Time in God's Word (Yes/No)**	**Rate Quality of Diet**	**Rate Overall Mood**
1					
2					
3					
4					
5					
6					
7					

Week _____ Ongoing Beginning Date:					
DAY	**Hours Slept**	**Minutes of Exercise**	**Time in God's Word (Yes/No)**	**Rate Quality of Diet**	**Rate Overall Mood**
1					
2					
3					
4					
5					
6					
7					

"Gospel Therapy"

Weeks 3 & 4 ~ Identifying My Uppers and Downers

Make a list like the one in the example below and keep it in a prominent place where you can refer to it regularly (or use the lists on the following pages). You may want to have a little diary book with you at all times to take notes, and then put them on this list later. Remember that an upper or downer isn't defined by what you feel like doing. Rather, an upper or downer is defined by what you feel like after doing something.

Classify each activity in the list as
P*=Physical* ***E****=Environmental* ***S****=Social Influence*

Physical: Walking, exercising, playing an instrument, napping, sleeping, gardening, eating, drinking, etc.

Environmental: Driving, being alone, being in crowds, at work, shopping, watching T.V., listening to music, reading, cooking, cleaning, etc.

Social: Work, family interaction, phone conversation, parties, school, attending athletic events, etc.

SAMPLE LIST

P ~ E ~ S	UPPERS	DOWNERS
P		Eating a pound of chocolate
P	Taking an evening walk	
S		Talking with my friend who likes to gossip
S	Talking with my children	
E		Watching T.V. by myself
E	Reading a book	

MY UPPER/DOWNER LIST

P ~ E ~ S	UPPERS	DOWNERS

MY UPPER/DOWNER LIST

P ~ E ~ S	UPPERS	DOWNERS

MY UPPER/DOWNER LIST

P ~ E ~ S	Uppers	Downers

MY UPPER/DOWNER LIST

P ~ E ~ S	UPPERS	DOWNERS

Analyzing Cognitive Distortions ~ Sample

Day: Sunday	**Cognitive Distortion (1-10):** VB: Jumping to Conclusions.
Describe Event: I got mad at the Pastor because he didn't shake my hand after church.	
Negative Fear, Doubt, Worry, or Guilt Associated with this Event: I am afraid of not being liked by people.	
Distorted or Negative Interpretation and Response That Was Made as a Result: I thought the Pastor was ignoring me, but the spouse of the person ahead of me had just died. The Pastor was just spending extra time with this person.	
Positive Aspect of God's Love and Promises That Answers Negative Feelings: I am truly loved by God. The more I focus on how much I am loved, the more I will focus on loving others, rather than worrying if they love me.	
More Appropriate Interpretation or Response Based on God's Grace: Tell the Pastor at an appropriate time how nice it is that he takes extra time greeting members who have special needs.	

Day: Wed.	**Cognitive Distortion (1-10):** VIII: Should Statements
Describe Event: Every time I think about my mother I feel sad. When she died I had gone to lunch and left her at the hospital. She died all alone while I was at lunch. I should have stayed. If I was there, maybe she wouldn't have died.	
Negative Fear, Doubt, Worry, or Guilt Associated with this Event: I feel guilty because I let my mother down, after she had done so much for me.	
Distorted or Negative Interpretation and Response That Was Made as a Result: Although I loved my mother very much I never feel happy when I think about her anymore.	
Positive Aspect of God's Love and Promises That Answers Negative Feelings: My mother is in heaven with Christ and feels nothing towards me except what he feels: forgiveness, love, and joy.	
More Appropriate Interpretation or Response Based on God's Grace: When I start to think about my mother I should not focus on what I did. Instead, I will focus on what Christ did for my mother, and everything he did for me through her.	

Analyzing Cognitive Distortions ~ Week 5

Day:	Cognitive Distortion (1-10):
Describe Event:	
Negative Fear, Doubt, Worry, or Guilt Associated with this Event:	
Distorted or Negative Interpretation and Response That Was Made as a Result:	
Positive Aspect of God's Love and Promises That Answers Negative Feelings:	
More Appropriate Interpretation or Response Based on God's Grace:	

Day:	Cognitive Distortion (1-10):
Describe Event:	
Negative Fear, Doubt, Worry, or Guilt Associated with this Event:	
Distorted or Negative Interpretation and Response That Was Made as a Result:	
Positive Aspect of God's Love and Promises That Answers Negative Feelings:	
More Appropriate Interpretation or Response Based on God's Grace:	

Analyzing Cognitive Distortions ~ Week 6 A

Day:	Cognitive Distortion (1-10):
Describe Event:	
Negative Fear, Doubt, Worry, or Guilt Associated with this Event:	
Distorted or Negative Interpretation and Response That Was Made as a Result:	
Positive Aspect of God's Love and Promises That Answers Negative Feelings:	
More Appropriate Interpretation or Response Based on God's Grace:	

Day:	Cognitive Distortion (1-10):
Describe Event:	
Negative Fear, Doubt, Worry, or Guilt Associated with this Event:	
Distorted or Negative Interpretation and Response That Was Made as a Result:	
Positive Aspect of God's Love and Promises That Answers Negative Feelings:	
More Appropriate Interpretation or Response Based on God's Grace:	

Analyzing Cognitive Distortions ~ Week 6 B

Day:	Cognitive Distortion (1-10):
Describe Event:	
Negative Fear, Doubt, Worry, or Guilt Associated with this Event:	
Distorted or Negative Interpretation and Response That Was Made as a Result:	
Positive Aspect of God's Love and Promises That Answers Negative Feelings:	
More Appropriate Interpretation or Response Based on God's Grace:	

Day:	Cognitive Distortion (1-10):
Describe Event:	
Negative Fear, Doubt, Worry, or Guilt Associated with this Event:	
Distorted or Negative Interpretation and Response That Was Made as a Result:	
Positive Aspect of God's Love and Promises That Answers Negative Feelings:	
More Appropriate Interpretation or Response Based on God's Grace:	

Analyzing Cognitive Distortions ~ Week 6 c

Day:	Cognitive Distortion (1-10):
Describe Event:	
Negative Fear, Doubt, Worry, or Guilt Associated with this Event:	
Distorted or Negative Interpretation and Response That Was Made as a Result:	
Positive Aspect of God's Love and Promises That Answers Negative Feelings:	
More Appropriate Interpretation or Response Based on God's Grace:	

Day:	Cognitive Distortion (1-10):
Describe Event:	
Negative Fear, Doubt, Worry, or Guilt Associated with this Event:	
Distorted or Negative Interpretation and Response That Was Made as a Result:	
Positive Aspect of God's Love and Promises That Answers Negative Feelings:	
More Appropriate Interpretation or Response Based on God's Grace:	

ANALYZING COGNITIVE DISTORTIONS ~ WEEK 7 A

Day:	Cognitive Distortion (1-10):
Describe Event:	
Negative Fear, Doubt, Worry, or Guilt Associated with this Event:	
Distorted or Negative Interpretation and Response That Was Made as a Result:	
Positive Aspect of God's Love and Promises That Answers Negative Feelings:	
More Appropriate Interpretation or Response Based on God's Grace:	

Day:	Cognitive Distortion (1-10):
Describe Event:	
Negative Fear, Doubt, Worry, or Guilt Associated with this Event:	
Distorted or Negative Interpretation and Response That Was Made as a Result:	
Positive Aspect of God's Love and Promises That Answers Negative Feelings:	
More Appropriate Interpretation or Response Based on God's Grace:	

Analyzing Cognitive Distortions ~ Week 7 b

Day:	**Cognitive Distortion (1-10):**
Describe Event:	
Negative Fear, Doubt, Worry, or Guilt Associated with this Event:	
Distorted or Negative Interpretation and Response That Was Made as a Result:	
Positive Aspect of God's Love and Promises That Answers Negative Feelings:	
More Appropriate Interpretation or Response Based on God's Grace:	

Day:	**Cognitive Distortion (1-10):**
Describe Event:	
Negative Fear, Doubt, Worry, or Guilt Associated with this Event:	
Distorted or Negative Interpretation and Response That Was Made as a Result:	
Positive Aspect of God's Love and Promises That Answers Negative Feelings:	
More Appropriate Interpretation or Response Based on God's Grace:	

ANALYZING COGNITIVE DISTORTIONS ~ WEEK 7 C

Day:	Cognitive Distortion (1-10):
Describe Event:	
Negative Fear, Doubt, Worry, or Guilt Associated with this Event:	
Distorted or Negative Interpretation and Response That Was Made as a Result:	
Positive Aspect of God's Love and Promises That Answers Negative Feelings:	
More Appropriate Interpretation or Response Based on God's Grace:	

Day:	Cognitive Distortion (1-10):
Describe Event:	
Negative Fear, Doubt, Worry, or Guilt Associated with this Event:	
Distorted or Negative Interpretation and Response That Was Made as a Result:	
Positive Aspect of God's Love and Promises That Answers Negative Feelings:	
More Appropriate Interpretation or Response Based on God's Grace:	

ANALYZING COGNITIVE DISTORTIONS ~ WEEK 8 A

Day:	Cognitive Distortion (1-10):
Describe Event:	
Negative Fear, Doubt, Worry, or Guilt Associated with this Event:	
Distorted or Negative Interpretation and Response That Was Made as a Result:	
Positive Aspect of God's Love and Promises That Answers Negative Feelings:	
More Appropriate Interpretation or Response Based on God's Grace:	

Day:	Cognitive Distortion (1-10):
Describe Event:	
Negative Fear, Doubt, Worry, or Guilt Associated with this Event:	
Distorted or Negative Interpretation and Response That Was Made as a Result:	
Positive Aspect of God's Love and Promises That Answers Negative Feelings:	
More Appropriate Interpretation or Response Based on God's Grace:	

ANALYZING COGNITIVE DISTORTIONS ~ WEEK 8 B

Day:	Cognitive Distortion (1-10):
Describe Event:	
Negative Fear, Doubt, Worry, or Guilt Associated with this Event:	
Distorted or Negative Interpretation and Response That Was Made as a Result:	
Positive Aspect of God's Love and Promises That Answers Negative Feelings:	
More Appropriate Interpretation or Response Based on God's Grace:	

Day:	Cognitive Distortion (1-10):
Describe Event:	
Negative Fear, Doubt, Worry, or Guilt Associated with this Event:	
Distorted or Negative Interpretation and Response That Was Made as a Result:	
Positive Aspect of God's Love and Promises That Answers Negative Feelings:	
More Appropriate Interpretation or Response Based on God's Grace:	

Analyzing Cognitive Distortions ~ Week 8 c

Day:	Cognitive Distortion (1-10):
Describe Event:	
Negative Fear, Doubt, Worry, or Guilt Associated with this Event:	
Distorted or Negative Interpretation and Response That Was Made as a Result:	
Positive Aspect of God's Love and Promises That Answers Negative Feelings:	
More Appropriate Interpretation or Response Based on God's Grace:	

Day:	Cognitive Distortion (1-10):
Describe Event:	
Negative Fear, Doubt, Worry, or Guilt Associated with this Event:	
Distorted or Negative Interpretation and Response That Was Made as a Result:	
Positive Aspect of God's Love and Promises That Answers Negative Feelings:	
More Appropriate Interpretation or Response Based on God's Grace:	

ANALYZING COGNITIVE DISTORTIONS ~ WEEK 9 A

Day:	Cognitive Distortion (1-10):
Describe Event:	
Negative Fear, Doubt, Worry, or Guilt Associated with this Event:	
Distorted or Negative Interpretation and Response That Was Made as a Result:	
Positive Aspect of God's Love and Promises That Answers Negative Feelings:	
More Appropriate Interpretation or Response Based on God's Grace:	

Day:	Cognitive Distortion (1-10):
Describe Event:	
Negative Fear, Doubt, Worry, or Guilt Associated with this Event:	
Distorted or Negative Interpretation and Response That Was Made as a Result:	
Positive Aspect of God's Love and Promises That Answers Negative Feelings:	
More Appropriate Interpretation or Response Based on God's Grace:	

ANALYZING COGNITIVE DISTORTIONS ~ WEEK 9 B

Day:	Cognitive Distortion (1-10):
Describe Event:	
Negative Fear, Doubt, Worry, or Guilt Associated with this Event:	
Distorted or Negative Interpretation and Response That Was Made as a Result:	
Positive Aspect of God's Love and Promises That Answers Negative Feelings:	
More Appropriate Interpretation or Response Based on God's Grace:	

Day:	Cognitive Distortion (1-10):
Describe Event:	
Negative Fear, Doubt, Worry, or Guilt Associated with this Event:	
Distorted or Negative Interpretation and Response That Was Made as a Result:	
Positive Aspect of God's Love and Promises That Answers Negative Feelings:	
More Appropriate Interpretation or Response Based on God's Grace:	

Analyzing Cognitive Distortions ~ Week 9 c

Day:	Cognitive Distortion (1-10):
Describe Event:	
Negative Fear, Doubt, Worry, or Guilt Associated with this Event:	
Distorted or Negative Interpretation and Response That Was Made as a Result:	
Positive Aspect of God's Love and Promises That Answers Negative Feelings:	
More Appropriate Interpretation or Response Based on God's Grace:	

Day:	Cognitive Distortion (1-10):
Describe Event:	
Negative Fear, Doubt, Worry, or Guilt Associated with this Event:	
Distorted or Negative Interpretation and Response That Was Made as a Result:	
Positive Aspect of God's Love and Promises That Answers Negative Feelings:	
More Appropriate Interpretation or Response Based on God's Grace:	

ANALYZING COGNITIVE DISTORTIONS ~ WEEK 10 A

Day:	Cognitive Distortion (1-10):
Describe Event:	
Negative Fear, Doubt, Worry, or Guilt Associated with this Event:	
Distorted or Negative Interpretation and Response That Was Made as a Result:	
Positive Aspect of God's Love and Promises That Answers Negative Feelings:	
More Appropriate Interpretation or Response Based on God's Grace:	

Day:	Cognitive Distortion (1-10):
Describe Event:	
Negative Fear, Doubt, Worry, or Guilt Associated with this Event:	
Distorted or Negative Interpretation and Response That Was Made as a Result:	
Positive Aspect of God's Love and Promises That Answers Negative Feelings:	
More Appropriate Interpretation or Response Based on God's Grace:	

Analyzing Cognitive Distortions ~ Week 10 b

Day:	Cognitive Distortion (1-10):
Describe Event:	
Negative Fear, Doubt, Worry, or Guilt Associated with this Event:	
Distorted or Negative Interpretation and Response That Was Made as a Result:	
Positive Aspect of God's Love and Promises That Answers Negative Feelings:	
More Appropriate Interpretation or Response Based on God's Grace:	

Day:	Cognitive Distortion (1-10):
Describe Event:	
Negative Fear, Doubt, Worry, or Guilt Associated with this Event:	
Distorted or Negative Interpretation and Response That Was Made as a Result:	
Positive Aspect of God's Love and Promises That Answers Negative Feelings:	
More Appropriate Interpretation or Response Based on God's Grace:	

Analyzing Cognitive Distortions ~ Week 10 c

Day:	Cognitive Distortion (1-10):
Describe Event:	
Negative Fear, Doubt, Worry, or Guilt Associated with this Event:	
Distorted or Negative Interpretation and Response That Was Made as a Result:	
Positive Aspect of God's Love and Promises That Answers Negative Feelings:	
More Appropriate Interpretation or Response Based on God's Grace:	

Day:	Cognitive Distortion (1-10):
Describe Event:	
Negative Fear, Doubt, Worry, or Guilt Associated with this Event:	
Distorted or Negative Interpretation and Response That Was Made as a Result:	
Positive Aspect of God's Love and Promises That Answers Negative Feelings:	
More Appropriate Interpretation or Response Based on God's Grace:	

Analyzing Cognitive Distortions ~ Ongoing Review

Day:	**Cognitive Distortion (1-10):**
Describe Event:	
Negative Fear, Doubt, Worry, or Guilt Associated with this Event:	
Distorted or Negative Interpretation and Response That Was Made as a Result:	
Positive Aspect of God's Love and Promises That Answers Negative Feelings:	
More Appropriate Interpretation or Response Based on God's Grace:	

Day:	**Cognitive Distortion (1-10):**
Describe Event:	
Negative Fear, Doubt, Worry, or Guilt Associated with this Event:	
Distorted or Negative Interpretation and Response That Was Made as a Result:	
Positive Aspect of God's Love and Promises That Answers Negative Feelings:	
More Appropriate Interpretation or Response Based on God's Grace:	

Analyzing Cognitive Distortions ~ Ongoing Review

Day:	Cognitive Distortion (1-10):
Describe Event:	
Negative Fear, Doubt, Worry, or Guilt Associated with this Event:	
Distorted or Negative Interpretation and Response That Was Made as a Result:	
Positive Aspect of God's Love and Promises That Answers Negative Feelings:	
More Appropriate Interpretation or Response Based on God's Grace:	

Day:	Cognitive Distortion (1-10):
Describe Event:	
Negative Fear, Doubt, Worry, or Guilt Associated with this Event:	
Distorted or Negative Interpretation and Response That Was Made as a Result:	
Positive Aspect of God's Love and Promises That Answers Negative Feelings:	
More Appropriate Interpretation or Response Based on God's Grace:	

Answer Guide to Lesson Study Questions

LESSON 1: UNDERSTANDING HOW THE BRAIN WORKS

Mark 12:30

With what four things are we to love our Lord? *Heart, soul, mind, strength.*

Psalm 31:9-10 and Proverbs 14:30

How do sorrow, grief, or envy affect our bodies? *My strength fails because of my affliction, and my bones grow weak. Envy rots the bones.*

Read Philippians 4:4-9

How does focusing on the good things in life affect our state of mind? *The God of peace will be with you.*

Read Jeremiah 31:31-34

Why did the old covenant God made with Israel fail? *Israel broke the covenant.*

How will God change Israel so that the new covenant will not fail? *God says, "I will put my law in their minds and write it on their hearts."*

Read Romans 12:2

What change must take place in order for us to be able to understand God's will? *Our minds must be renewed.*

Read Mark 1:14-15

What kind of news does Jesus bring to us? *Good news.*

What change occurs with those who repent? *They believe good news.*

Lesson 3: The Effects of Lifestyle and Activities on Our Minds

Read Psalm 127:1-2 and Ecclesiastes 5:10-12

What does a lack of sleep suggest about our priorities? *We are too worried about earthly and material matters.*

Read Proverbs 3:21-26 and Ecclesiastes 2:22-26

How does trust in God affect our ability to sleep? *The more we trust in him to care for us the easier it will be for us to sleep*

Read Isaiah 30:15-16

Where is our salvation found? *In repentance and rest*

What prevents Israel from experiencing God's salvation? *They don't want God's help.*

Read Genesis 2:18

Is it good for us to be alone? *No, God created us to be with others.*

Read Psalm 32:3-6 and 39:2-3

How does silence affect the body and the spirit? *Silence is not good for our heart or soul.*

Read Isaiah 38:18-19

Why is life better than death? *It gives us an opportunity to praise God and talk about his faithfulness.*

Lesson 4: Thinking Styles and Their Effects on the Brain

What are the possible explanations for the people not waving back? *They are ignoring me. They are mad at me. They didn't see me. They didn't recognize me.*

Putting the "best construction" on everything, of the above possibilities which would you pick? *They didn't see me.*

Using the "worst case scenario," which of the above possibilities would you pick? *They are mad at me.*

What reasons did you write down earlier for not stealing? *Most people say that it's wrong, it's against the commandments, or something similar.*

Read Matthew 6:24-34 and Hebrews 13:5-6

What motive does God supply to us to prevent us from being tempted with money or material things? *God will watch over us and take care of us.*

Based on the verses above, how would you now respond to the question "Why should Christians not steal?" *I don't have to steal because God will take care of me.*

Lesson 5: The Mental Distortions That Conflict With God's World View

Read Romans 1:16-17, Acts 20:24, and 1 Corinthians 15:1-4

Write down a working definition of the gospel. *The power of God for salvation found in testifying to his grace in Jesus Christ who died and rose to pay for our sins.*

Read Romans 1:17

What principle should determine the righteous actions of Christians in this world? *Christians should live by faith in the gospel.*

Read Romans 6:14, Galatians 3:12 and 5:18

Should Christians live by God's law or by God's grace? *Christians should live by God's grace.*

Read Luke 23:39-43

What is this criminal's immediate future on earth? *He will die.*

What is this criminal's eternal future if it is true that *"good people go to heaven and bad people go to hell?"* *He will go to hell.*

How is this criminal's eternal future changed by the gospel of forgiveness purchased through Christ? *He is guaranteed a place in heaven.*

Read Romans 3:19-24; 5:20-21; 7:7-13

Can we become righteous by obeying the law? *No.*

Then why did God give us the law? *God gave us the law to make us more aware of our sinfulness.*

Was the doctor acting appropriately when he administered the tests he gave to you? *Yes!*

In what ways has this doctor failed to do his job? *He didn't tell me what kind of sickness I had nor did he tell me how to be cured.*

Read Mark 2:23-28

How did the Pharisees understand the Sabbath? *They thought it was an obligation that we must keep to please God.*

How did Jesus understand the Sabbath? *Jesus taught that the Sabbath was a gift of God to us.*

Read Acts 2:37-39; 22:16; Ephesians 5:25-27

What is the function of baptism? *Wash away our sins.*

If baptism does what the Bible says, what has happened to the sins of the baptized person? *They have been taken away and the person has become holy and blameless.*

Can the baptized person in some way speak of themself as being perfect? *Yes, through Christ.*

Lesson 6: The Distortions of "All or Nothing" and "Over-Generalization"

Read Matthew 5:44-48

What standard of achievement does God have for us? *We must be perfect.*

Read Galatians 5:19-21

What is the penalty for failing to live according to God's standards? *We will not inherit the kingdom of God.*

Read Romans 3:10-20 and Isaiah 64:6

Can anyone achieve perfection on their own? *No.*

Do any of our deeds measure up to God's standards of righteousness? *No.*

Read Romans 3:21-28

How does a person become righteous? *We are justified or made righteous through faith in Christ without observing the law.*

Read Galatians 5:22-25

How is life under the Spirit different from life under the law? *We experience the fruits of love, joy, peace, etc.*

Read Luke 18:18-27

What question does this rich ruler ask of Jesus? *What must I do to inherit eternal life?*

Did this rich ruler think that he was living a good life? *Yes.*

What caused the rich ruler to become depressed? *When Jesus said, "Sell everything you have and give to the poor, and you will have treasure in heaven."*

What is impossible for us? *We cannot save ourselves.*

What is possible for God? *God can save us.*

Read Psalm 18:32; 51:7; Colossians 1:28; Revelation 7:13-14 and Hebrews 10:11-14

What is our condition in Christ Jesus? *Cleansed of all sin and perfect.*

Can you, in some way, say that you are perfect? *Yes.*

Read Psalm 14:2-3 and Romans 3:10-12

From God's point of view is there anyone who naturally seeks him? *Nobody seeks him or does what is good.*

Read Romans 7:18-19

Does the apostle Paul see himself as capable of doing anything right? *He wants to do good but keeps on doing evil.*

Read Romans 8:24-28

In what things is God at work for good? *All things.*

What is the "good" for which God works? (See also Matthew 6:33) *The good of those who love him and have been called according to his purpose.*

Read Matthew 5:3-12

What "negative" experiences are called blessed? *Those who are poor in spirit, who mourn, who are meek, who are persecuted because of righteousness.*

Read 1 Corinthians 1:23-31

Who does God choose as his witnesses? *The foolish things, the weak things, the lowly things, and the despised things of this world.*

Read Philippians 1:12-14

What is the negative in Paul's life? *He is chained up for the sake of Christ.*

How has this negative become a positive? *He can preach to the palace guard and his chains have encouraged others to speak the word more courageously and fearlessly.*

Read Philippians 1:15-18

What is the negative in Paul's life? *Some preach Christ out of envy and rivalry and to stir up trouble.*

How has this negative become a positive? *In every way, whether from false motives or true, Christ is preached.*

Read Philippians 1:20-26

What two possibilities face the apostle Paul? *Life on earth or death.*

Why is neither possibility seen as a negative? *Life means fruitful labor for Christ and death means going to heaven.*

Read Philippians 4:6

What does every prayer of the apostle Paul include? *Thanksgiving.*

Read John 9:1-12, 35-39

What were the only two explanations for this man's blindness offered by the disciples? *Either he sinned or his parents sinned.*

What explanation for this blindness did Jesus offer? *This happened so that the work of God might be displayed in his life.*

Besides being cured of blindness, what positive results grew out of this man being born blind? *He told others about Jesus.*

Read 2 Corinthians 12:6-9

Did Paul initially understand this thorn as a blessing? *No.*

What was Paul's initial prayer regarding this thorn? *Paul wanted God to take the thorn away.*

How did God's revelation change Paul's attitude toward this thorn? *He saw it as something to boast about.*

Lesson 7: The Distortions of "Mental Filters" and "Disqualifying the Positive"

Read Philippians 4:8-9

What should be the focus of our thoughts? *Anything that is excellent or praiseworthy.*

What is the result of this kind of focus in our life? *God's peace will be with us.*

Read 1 Corinthians 13:4-7

What does love focus on in other people? *It focuses on their good points rather than their bad points.*

Read Matthew 20:1-15

How do you think the workers hired first initially felt when they got a job? *They felt grateful because they were unemployed.*

What change in mental focus caused the workers hired first to become upset? *They saw people who worked far less than them getting the same pay and thought they deserved more money.*

How did the landowner's interpretation of his actions differ from the workers' interpretation? *He saw himself as gracious, they saw him as being unfair.*

Read 1 Corinthians 15:9

Did Paul deserve to be called an apostle? *No, because he had persecuted the church.*

Read 1 Timothy 1:14-16

With 1 being very bad and 10 being very good, where would Paul place himself on a "goodness" scale? *Number 1: Paul saw himself as the worst of sinners.*

Why would God pick Paul to be his servant? *To display his unlimited patience as an example for those who would believe on him and receive eternal life.*

Read Romans 7:14-25

What happens when Paul tries to do something good? *He ends up doing something evil.*

Read 1 Thessalonians 5:18; Colossians 3:17; and Ephesians 5:19-20

When should we be thankful to God? *In all circumstances all the time.*

Read Galatians 6:14; 1 Corinthians 1:27-31

What should Christians boast about? *They should boast about God and the cross of Jesus Christ.*

Lesson 8: The Distortions of "Jumping to Conclusions" Through "Mind Reading" or "Negative Prediction"

Read Galatians 1:8-10; 2:5-6 and 1 Thessalonians 2:4

What governed the way the apostle Paul behaved? *He was only interested in pleasing God.*

Read 1 Corinthians 4:3-5

What weight does Paul place on the judgments of others in determining his behavior? *None.*

Though not specifically stated, why do you think Paul is not afraid of the Lord's judgment, even though he is "not innocent?" *Because he knows that Christ has already taken care of his faults.*

Read 1 John 3:13-20

What impact should the world "hating" us have on our Christian behavior? *None.*

What forms the basis of our love for others? *The fact that Jesus laid down his life for us.*

Read Romans 12:19-21 and Proverbs 20:22

Why is "revenge" a non-issue for Christians? *Because God will take care of it.*

How does the Christian deal with evil and why? *We deal with evil by doing good so that we may overcome it.*

Read Titus 2:9-10

Why should slaves try to please their masters? *To make the teaching about Christ attractive.*

Read Ecclesiastes 2:17-23; 5:12-17

What do we get for all our human efforts? *Grief and no rest.*

Read Ecclesiastes 12:12-14

What is the "bottom line" of what we should be doing during our life on this earth? *Fear God and keep his commandments.*

Read John 15:5-6

Without Christ, what can we accomplish? *Nothing.*

With Christ, what can we accomplish? *We will bear much fruit.*

Read Philippians 4:10-13

In what situations can the apostle Paul be content? *Whatever circumstances he finds himself in.*

What is Paul's secret to contentment? *He knows he can do everything through Christ who gives him strength.*

Read Ephesians 1:7-10

What is God's ultimate purpose for the world? *To bring all things together under Christ.*

Read Matthew 28:18-20

What is the goal of Christ's authority ? *To make disciples of all nations.*

Read 1 Corinthians 1:25-31

What kind of people are God's first choice in witnessing to this world? *Not those of noble birth or those considered wise in the world's eyes, but the lowly and despised.*

Read Matthew 5:1-12

Would you consider the "blessed" people in these passages "successful" from this world's viewpoint? *No.*

Lesson 9: The Distortions of "Magnification" or "Minimization" and "Emotional Reasoning"

Read Romans 10:9-13 and Acts 2:38

What objective truth do these Bible passages teach about who will be saved? *If you believe Jesus died for you and that he is your Lord, you will be saved.*

Based on these Bible passages and her confession of Christ, where would this woman go if she died? *To heaven.*

Read Romans 7:21-25; 8:5-11

How many minds live inside of the Christian? *Two*

What are the two minds or spirits? *The sinful nature and the spirit of Christ.*

What does the sinful nature (flesh) always want to do? *Sinful things which show hostility to God.*

What does the Spirit of Christ always want to do? *Spiritual things which please God.*

Read John 8:31-34 and Romans 8:13-16

What is life lived in sin? *Slavery to sin and fear.*

What is life lived in the spirit? *Freedom.*

Read 1 John 4:15-19

What is perfect love and where does it come from? *Love without fear which comes from God's love for us.*

Should fear be a part of our response to the world? *No.*

Lesson 10: The Distortions of "Should Statements" and "Labeling"

Read Genesis 28:12-17

v. 15 What promises does Jacob receive from God? *Land, many descendants, other people will be blessed through you, and God will watch over Jacob wherever he goes and bring him back.*

v. 16 What does Jacob learn about God's presence? *God was present with him, even when he didn't know it.*

Read Matthew 28:18-20 and Hebrews 13:5

What promise have we received from Christ? *The promise that he is always with us.*

Read Psalm 139:1-10

Is there a place where God's hand cannot reach? *There is no place we can be where God cannot reach us.*

Read Luke 18:9-14

Why does Jesus tell this parable? (see v. 9) *Some people were confident of their righteousness and looked down on everyone else.*

Who is denied forgiveness and how would he label himself? *The Pharisee who thought he was a very good person.*

Who is given forgiveness and how would he label himself? *The tax collector who thought he was a very bad person.*

Lesson 11: The Distortion of "Personalization"

Read Psalm 41:4-9 and 69:1-4

How did David see the world around him? *Everybody is out to destroy him.*

Read Psalm 41:10-13 and Psalm 69:6, 33-36

What certainty does David cling to in the midst of his despair? *God will raise him up and uphold him. God will save his people.*

Read Psalm 56:3-4 and Psalm 118:5-6

Why is David unafraid of what others can do to him? *He places his trust in God who is with him and will help him.*

Read Romans 8:31-39

Who can separate us from God's love? *Nothing can separate us from God's love.*

Read John 10:27-29

What promise does Jesus give with regard to all of his sheep? *No one can snatch them out of my Father's hand.*

Read Ezekiel 18:20-23

If someone perishes, whose fault is it? *Their own fault.*

Read Esther 4:6-16

According to verse 14, what does Mordecai believe will happen to the Jews if Esther fails to act? *Relief and deliverance for the Jews will arise from another place.*

What does Mordecai believe is the reason Esther became a queen? *She came to her royal position for such a time as this.*

Is Esther worried that she might be killed and fail? *No. "If I perish, I perish."*

Read 1 Corinthians 10:13

What promise does God make to us in this verse? *He will not let us be tempted beyond what we can bear, but will always provide a way out.*

Why might belief in the first part of this verse be essential to believing in the promise? *Sometimes we think our problems our so unique that we don't listen to the counsel God might offer to us through others.*

Read Hebrews 2:14 - 3:1 and Hebrews 4:14-16

Why did God's Son take on human flesh? *To make us more confident that he understands and sympathizes with our weaknesses.*

Read 2 Corinthians 4:5-7

Through what vehicle does God reveal his glory? *Jars of clay.*

Read 1 Timothy 1:15-16

Why did God choose Paul as his witness? *So that God could display his unlimited patience.*

Read Titus 2:9-10 and 1 Peter 2:18-21

Why should slaves be submissive to harsh masters? *To make the teaching about God our Savior attractive.*

Read 1 Peter 3:1-3

Why should wives be submissive to husbands who are not believers? *So they can be won over without words by the behavior of their wives.*

Scripture Verse Index

KEY CODE: L=Lesson W=Weekly Activities INT=Introduction